OTIEICTONAIWNATOEAEOCAYTY
ENXEIPIKPATAIAKAIENBPAXIONIYYH
OTIEICTONAIWNATOEAEOCXH
TWKATAAIEAONTITHNEPYOPAN
OAAACCANEICAIEPECEIC
OTIEICTONAIWNATOEAEOCXH
KAIAINAIONTITONICXENMECWAYTH
OTIEICTONAIWNATOEAEOCXY
KAIEKTINAZANTIФAPAWKAITHNAYNA
MINAYTOYEICOAAACCANEPYOPA
OTIEICTONAIWNATOEAEOCXYOY
TWAINAIONTITONAAONAYTOYENHHE
OTIEICTONAIWNATOEAEOCXY
TWПATAZANTIBACIAEICMEIAAOYC
OTIEICTONAIWNATOEAEOCXH
KAIAПOKTINANTIBACIAEICKPATAIOYC
OTIEICTONAIWNATOEAEOCXY
TONCHWNBACIAEATWNAMOPPAIWN
OTIEICTONAIWNATOEAEOCXY
KAITONWIBACIAEATHCBACAN
OTIEICTONAIWNATOEAEOCXY
KAIAONTITHNIHNAYTWNKAHPON WH
OTIEICTONAIWNATOEAEOCXH
KAHPONOMIANIHAAOYAWAYTOY
OTIEICTONAIWNATOEAEOCXY
KAIEAYTPWCATOHMACEKXIPOC
EXOPWNHMWN
OTIEICTONAIWNATOEAEOCXY
OAIAOYCTPOФHNПACHCAPKI
OTIEICTONAIWNATOEAEOCXY
EZOMOAOГEICOEOTWTOYOYPANY
OTIEICTONAIWNATOEAEOCXY
IWAAA
EПITWNПOTAMWNBABYAWNOC
EKEIEKAOICAMENKAIEKAAYCAM
ENTWMNHCOHNAIHMACTHCCIW
EПITAICITEAICENMECWAYTHC
EKPEMACAMENTAOPГANAHMWN
OTIEKEHPWTHCANHMACOIAIXMA
AWTEYCANTECHMACAOГOYC
KAIOIAПAГAГONTECHMACYMNTHX
HMINEKTWNWAWNCIWN
ПWCACWMENTHNWAHNKYEПIГHC
AAAOTPIAC
EANEПIAAOWMAICOYIHAMEПI
AHCOIHHAEZIAMOY
KOAAHOEIHHГAWCCAMOYTWAAPTI
ГIMOYEANMHCOYMNHCOW

OTIENTHTAПINWCEIHMWNEMNHCOHHMWNOKCOTIEICTONAI
WNATOEAEOCAYTOY

EANMHПPOANATAZWMAITHNIHAM
ENAPXHTHCEYФPOCYNHCM
MNHCOHTIKETWNYIWNEAWM
THNHMEPANIHAM
TWNAEГONTWNEKKENOYTEEKKEN
TAIEWCOYOEMEAIOCENAYTHC
OYГATHPBABYAWNOCHTAAAIПWPO
MAKAPIOCOCANTAПOAWCICOITON
ПTAПOAOMACOYOANTAПEAWKANHI
MAKAPIOCOCKPATHCEIKAIEAAФIEI
TANHПIACOYПPOCTHNПETPAN
IWAAA
PAZEZOMOAOГHCOMAICOIKEENOAH
KAPAIAMOY
OTIHKOYCACTAPHMAIATOYCTOMATY
KAIENANTIONAГГEAWNYAAWCOI
ПPOCKYNHCWПPOCNAONAГION
COYKAIEZOMOAOГHCOMAI
TWONOMATICOY
EПITWEAEEICOYKAITHNAAHOIACOY
OTIEMEГAAYNACEПIПANONOMA
TOAГIONCOY
ENHANHMEPAEПIKAAECWMAIOC
TAXYEПAKOYCONMOY
ПOAYWPHCEICMEENYXHMOY
ENAYNAMIПOAAICOY
EZOMOAOГHCACOWCANCOIKE
ПANTECOIBACIAEICTHCГHC
OTIHKOYCANПANTATAPHMATA
TOYCTOMATOCCOY
KAIACATWCANENTAICOAOICKY
OTIHAOZAKYMEIAAH
OTIYЧHAOCKCKAITATAПINAEФOPA
KAITAYЧHAAAПOMAKPOOENГINWK
EANПOPEYOWMENMECWOAIYE
WZHCEICME
EПOPГHNEXOPWNEZETINAXEIPAC
KAIECWCENMEHAEZIACOY
KCANTAПOAWCEICYПEPEMOY
KCTOEAEOCCOYEICTONAIWNA
KCTAEPГATWNXIPWNCOYMHПAPIA
EICTOTEAOCЧAAMOCTWAAA
PAHKEEAOKIMACACMEKAIEГNWCME
CYEГNWCTHNKAOEAPANMOY
KAITHNEГEPCINMOY
CYCYNHKACПANTACTOYCAIAAOГICM
MOYAПOMAKPOOEN
THNTPIBONMOYKAITHNCXOINON

CODEX SINAITICUS

The Story of the World's Oldest Bible

CODEX SINAITICUS

The Story of the World's Oldest Bible

D. C. PARKER

THE BRITISH LIBRARY

HENDRICKSON

First published 2010 by
The British Library
96 Euston Road
London NW1 2DB
and
Hendrickson Publishers, Inc.
PO Box 3473
Peabody
Massachusetts 01961-3473

ISBN 978-1-59856-576-8 (Hendrickson Publishers)
ISBN 978-0-7123-5803-3 (The British Library)

A CIP record for this book is available from The British Library and the Library of Congress

Designed by Bob Elliott
Typeset by Norman Tilley Graphics Ltd, Northampton
Printed in Hong Kong by Great Wall Printing Co.

CONTENTS

LIST OF ILLUSTRATIONS

Front endpaper: Psalms 133 to 136 in Codex Sinaiticus (Quire 63, Folios 5v–6r). An illustration containing the first verse of Psalm 133 seemed appropriate for a project involving many partners: 'Behold how good and how pleasant it is for brethren to dwell together in unity!'

Back endpaper: John 6.23–7.18 (Quire 80, Folios 4v–5r), containing Jesus' 'bread of life' discourse.

BLACK AND WHITE DECORATIONS

FOREWORD

IT IS a story that could be told in many different ways. When it begins, where it begins, even what happened, are all matters for debate. This telling begins in London at six o'clock in the evening on 9 March 2005. The place is the British Library, and a document is to be signed by four representatives: the Archbishop of Sinai, the Chief Executive of the British Library, the Director of Leipzig University Library and the Deputy Director of the National Library of Russia, St Petersburg. They have come to sign their commitment to collaborate in researching and making globally accessible one of the most remarkable and famous of all manuscripts, a fourth-century copy of the Bible in Greek which is called Codex Sinaiticus. This book is one of the results of that agreement, and I am grateful to the Codex Sinaiticus Project Board for inviting me to write it.

It is customary for an author to express his gratitude to those who have helped him travel the long and stony road from the first blank sheet of paper to the published book. Such appreciation is particularly appropriate for a work which is one part of a large project. Many people have spent six years with Codex Sinaiticus, and I have bothered an unconscionable number of them for information. Some of them have played especially important roles in sending me in the right direction to find materials, sharing unpublished research with me and answering questions. Their help is acknowledged at the end of each chapter. At the British Library, I am above all indebted to Scot McKendrick, and after him to Claire Breay and more recently Juan Garcés, for their advice and encouragement. Father Justin of St

Catherine's Monastery, Sinai, has always been most generous with his expertise. Dr Nicholas Fyssas of the Mount Sinai Foundation, Athens made a major contribution to Chapters 9 and 10 by making available to me his report on the monastery's documentation concerning the Codex and by further information, including a number of the texts.

In Birmingham, the members of the team which made the transcription of Codex Sinaiticus (Amy Myshrall, Tim Brown, Rachel Kevern and Hugh Houghton) have not only produced much of the raw data which I have used, but also responded to numerous questions and suggestions.

The typescript was read by a number of people who offered valuable comments, each in a particular way, including Hugh Houghton, Tim Brown, Ulrich Johannes Schneider, Ekaterina Krushelnitskaya, Karen Parker and T. H. L. Parker. Richard Jones exceeded the call even of long friendship in the care shown by his discerning comments about the book's tone and structure.

Finally, my thanks are due to David Way, Publisher at the British Library, for his support and encouragement.

This book was commissioned by the Codex Sinaiticus Project Board. Throughout the work I have been at pains to take into account the aims of the Project and its spirit. But it is my book, and whatever errors there are, they are mine.

D. C. PARKER

Bromyard, Herefordshire
February 2010

A SIMPLE EXPLANATION

CODEX SINAITICUS is a Latin name. 'Codex' means a particular kind of book, the book as we know it, consisting of a number of sheets folded in half, written on both sides and joined together with thread. 'Sinaiticus' means 'Sinaitic' ('of Sinai' or 'from Sinai'). The reference is to Sinai in Egypt. There is a long tradition of naming manuscripts after places with which they are associated, but the name does not necessarily indicate either where a manuscript was written or where it is now. In English, 'The book from Sinai' is at once too imprecise and too definite. The 'Sinaitic manuscript' is a better translation. Codex is pronounced with a long o (as in 'code'). Sinaiticus is pronounced 'sigh-nay-itty-cuss'; the stress lies on the third syllable.

CHAPTER ONE

Every Book its Destiny

The title of this
chapter is taken
from the line by
the second-century
Latin grammarian
Terentianus
Maurus: *Habent
sua fata libelli.*

ODEX SINAITICUS is one of the greatest of all books, not only as a Christian production, but within all human culture and book technology. A manuscript containing the whole Bible in Greek, it was made in the middle of the fourth century, in the south-eastern Mediterranean. It is written on parchment, and originally contained upwards of 740 leaves, or 1,480 pages. It stands alone as the oldest surviving complete New Testament, and is one of the two oldest manuscripts of the whole Bible. The fourth century was a vital period in the development of Christianity, in the preservation of the Christian Scriptures and in the development of the book. Codex Sinaiticus is our greatest written witness to this epoch. It is to Christian books what Hagia Sophia is to Christian buildings. The same Byzantine confidence created them; each is incomparably beautiful; together they represent the enduring significance of their age.

See Plate 1

This book tells the story of the manuscript's making and the world in which it was made, of its use in the ancient world and its modern history, of the texts which it contains and the modern Project (the capital letter singles it out) which has recreated it virtually.

A SHORT HISTORY OF CODEX SINAITICUS

Its copying

The manuscript was copied by a team of at least three scribes. Of these one was the most expert and senior, one copied the most and

Of the various places called Caesarea, this book always refers to Caesarea Maritima in Palestine.

one was the least satisfactory. The scribes revised and corrected their work. The place where this happened is unknown, but it is most likely to have been either Caesarea or Egypt. As to contents, the Old Testament contained the forty-eight books of the Greek canon, in the translation called the Septuagint, and the New Testament has the twenty-seven books found in the most widely accepted canon, followed by two other early Christian writings, the Epistle of Barnabas and the Shepherd of Hermas. Among Greek manuscripts, it is by five hundred years the oldest complete New Testament to have survived, the oldest complete copy of Hebrews, the Pastoral Epistles, Philemon and Revelation, and one of the two oldest complete copies of the Gospels, Acts and Catholic Epistles. It is by far the oldest copy of the Epistle of Barnabas. It is one of the two oldest copies of the Old Testament.

The technical challenges of making this book were considerable, and the scribes emerge with credit. Its page size remains the largest of any surviving Greek biblical manuscript, and at the same time the parchment is some of the thinnest ever used. It is beautifully written, in the script known as biblical majuscule.

The text

As in every manuscript, the wording of the texts of Codex Sinaiticus is unique. Sometimes these are changes, mostly accidental but occasionally intended, by the scribes. Others had been introduced into previous copies. Because it is such an ancient copy, the study of these differences in wording is very important for understanding how the books which it contains were copied in antiquity. This study has two aspects to it. One is the attempt to recover as old as possible a wording. Such a wording will never be identical with the original wording of the author (or translator in the case of the Septuagint), but represents the closest one can get on the basis of the available evidence. The other aspect is to study the ways in which the various manuscripts differ from each other and from the oldest recoverable wording. This helps us to understand how early Christian groups and individuals read and altered the text.

Its use in antiquity

From about fifty years after its creation, for a period which lasted till around 600, the Codex was extensively revised by a succession of correctors. There are nearly 23,000 revisions (at an overall average of almost thirty on each page). Such a number is unique among ancient manuscripts. The majority were carried out by six correctors. Their work included rewriting faded letters, correcting spelling, changing the way in which words are broken across lines and inserting omitted text. They also changed wording and sometimes deleted material.

At some point the manuscript was removed to St Catherine's Monastery, Sinai. The oldest Christian monastery in the world, St Catherine's was founded by the Emperor Justinian in the middle of the sixth century. We do not know when the manuscript arrived there, but there is no reason to doubt that it was at quite an early stage (before the year 1000, in all probability). Certainly there are medieval Greek marginal notes which indicate that it was in a monastic environment, while the presence of several comments in Arabic also suggests a setting consonant with St Catherine's.

See Plate 2

Its modern history

The history of the manuscript down to the eighteenth century is not known. How much it was used and in what way we cannot tell. There is evidence that pieces of it were used as a source of material for bookbinding in the late eighteenth and early nineteenth centuries. From 1844 the story can be told in detail. In that year a German scholar from Leipzig called Constantin Tischendorf was shown some leaves of the Old Testament, and allowed to take forty-three of them home with him. These leaves are in Leipzig University Library. The following year a Russian monk, Porphyry Uspenski, visited Sinai. He found some fragments of the manuscript which had been used for bookbinding, and took them back to St Petersburg. Tischendorf returned in 1859, and all of the manuscript that was then known to survive was shown to him, and subsequently loaned for a complete copy to be made. After protracted negotiations these pages became the property of Tsar Alexander II of Russia in 1869.

Tischendorf published the leaves acquired in 1844 shortly after his return, in an edition which imitated the page layout of the manuscript and reproduced the appearance of the characters with specially made type. After the 1859 visit, he made a similar edition of the entire manuscript, which was presented to the Tsar and Tsarina in 1862. Both these editions include information about every correction, indicating both the original wording and what replaced it, and which corrector made it.

Superb though these editions were, the publication of a photographic facsimile in the early years of the last century was a significant improvement, the New Testament being published in 1911 and the Old Testament in 1922. The scholarly part of the work was carried out by the British scholar Kirsopp Lake and his wife Helen. They re-examined Tischendorf's theories with regard to the scribes and correctors, accepting them so far as the scribes were concerned, but elaborating the list of correctors. The facsimile itself has served fairly well, in spite of the weakness that it is not in colour, and is sometimes rather grey in tone.

Kirsopp Lake (1872–1946) trained in Oxford and was professor at Leiden when the first volume came out and at Harvard on the publication of the second.

The manuscript stayed in St Petersburg until 1933, when it was bought by the British Museum for £100,000. It arrived in London on 26 December, and went on view on 28 December. Rebound by the distinguished bookbinder Douglas Cockerell, it was the subject of a detailed analysis by two Assistant Keepers of Manuscripts, H. J. M. Milne and T. C. Skeat. They assessed the contributions of Tischendorf and the Lakes, and came to new and convincing conclusions with regard to both scribes and correctors. Their work also includes copious illustrations, and discussion of many important matters concerning the book's creation and preservation. It

4

focuses on the physical aspects, and has very little to say about the text itself.

The manuscript was on show in the Manuscripts Saloon until the British Library was moved to a new building at St Pancras in 1998. There it may still be seen in the Sir John Ritblat Gallery, flanked by another famous Greek Bible and amongst many other wonderful manuscripts: Bibles in Greek and Latin (such as the Lindisfarne Gospels) and other languages; the fourteenth-century Sultan Baybar's Qur'an in seven stunning volumes; service and prayer books such as the Sherborne Missal and the Golden Haggadah; literary texts and musical scores such as Handel's *Messiah*; notes and sketches by Leonardo da Vinci; political documents, most notably Magna Carta. Among this display, which illustrates creative genius, world history and the highest achievements in book manufacture, Codex Sinaiticus continues to hold its own as one of the most significant copies of one of the most significant bodies of text ever to have been produced.

Meanwhile, in 1975 a remarkable event occurred at St Catherine's: the discovery of a room containing many manuscripts and fragments of manuscripts, including complete and partial leaves of Codex Sinaiticus. These leaves have only recently been published, as part of the Virtual Codex Sinaiticus.

Summary

The surviving parts of the Codex are therefore:

eighty-six pages in Leipzig
694 pages in London
portions of eight pages in St Petersburg
some or all of thirty-six pages in St Catherine's

Two pages are shared between London and St Petersburg.

THE CODEX SINAITICUS PROJECT

The significance of Codex Sinaiticus led Tischendorf and his patrons to produce magnificent print facsimiles. In the same way the Virtual

Codex Sinaiticus seeks to attain the highest standards in electronic technology, providing high-resolution digital images, detailed records of the parchment of every page, transcriptions of the text and other descriptive and interpretative materials. It has also a further goal, which was beyond the reach of both the makers of the manuscript and the print and photographic facsimiles, namely access for all. The World Wide Web offers an up-to-date presentation of the whole of Codex Sinaiticus, virtually reunited, globally at no cost to anyone with a browser.

In addition to the website, the four Project Partners agreed to commission research which would lead to their endorsing an agreed account of the circumstances under which parts of the manuscript were removed from St Catherine's, in particular those leaves which were taken to St Petersburg. This research has included examination of the relevant documentation in St Petersburg, Moscow, Leipzig and St Catherine's.

Recent developments in access to texts is as significant as the Gutenberg revolution. Printing with movable type, introduced in western Europe in the fifteenth century, made books far cheaper and easier to produce than manuscript copies could ever be. Publication on the internet goes even further in creating new readerships.

Further goals of the Project have been a conference (held at the British Library in July 2009), a book making the Project and its findings accessible to a wide audience (you are holding it), and a print facsimile edition.

These are ambitious goals. They are yet another indication of the high significance of Codex Sinaiticus. So far as the website is concerned, they mark a new departure in manuscript study. It will never be possible to obtain this level of information in editions of any but the most important manuscripts. The Project is a statement of what can be achieved today with something which amply deserves such treatment. This is the story of Codex Sinaiticus. A production of unique quality; corrected in antiquity more extensively and with more care than any other manuscript; edited in a typographic facsimile in the production of which no expense was spared in the middle of the nineteenth century; edited digitally today in a project which has set new standards in professional conservation and scholarly research.

The Project has generated material which it will take scholars many years to study in detail. What follows, an introduction to Codex Sinaiticus, offers some a way of taking stock of the Project, and others an invitation to explore the world of Greek texts and Greek manuscripts.

CODEX SINAITICUS IN OUTLINE

The following summary statements about the manuscript may be useful for reference.

Names:	The whole manuscript is known as Codex Sinaiticus (in the nineteenth century it was called Codex Sinaiticus Petropolitanus; the Petropolitanus was generally ignored, and certainly abandoned by the end of 1933); the Leipzig leaves used to be called Codex Friderico-Augustanus
Date:	Around the middle of the fourth century
Place of origin:	Somewhere in Asia Minor, Palestine (Caesarea?) or Egypt
Written by:	At least three scribes
Writing material:	Animal skin (calf and sheep)
Ink:	Black (metallic base) and red
Language:	Greek (with several Arabic marginal notes added much later)
Number of leaves (originally):	
	743 (1486 pages)
(wholly or partially surviving):	
	411 (822 pages), excluding fragments too small for the text to be identified

The calculation assumes an initial quire of four leaves (8 pages) and that Hermas was the last book in the Codex.

Page size: 43 cm wide by 38 cm high (16.9 inches by 15)

Number of columns per page:

Four (two in the poetical and wisdom literature)

Number of lines per column (normally):

Forty-eight

Current locations: London, British Library, Additional Manuscript 43725 (the majority of the manuscript, including all the New Testament)

Leipzig, University Library, Codices graeci I (part of 1 Chronicles, all of 2 Esdras and Esther, a page of Tobit, part of Jeremiah and what survives of Lamentations)

St Petersburg, National Library of Russia, Codices graeci 2, 259, 843, Oct. 156 (fragments from Genesis, Numbers, Judith and Hermas)

Sinai, Monastery of St Catherine, New Finds (sections and fragments of Genesis, Leviticus, Numbers, Deuteronomy, Joshua, Judges, 1 Chronicles and Hermas)

Contents (originally):

The Old Testament (according to the canon of the Greek Septuagint, including the books which are known in English as the Apocrypha, but without 2 and 3 Maccabees), the New Testament and two other early Christian books (the Shepherd of Hermas and the Epistle of Barnabas).[1]

Contents (today):   *Partially surviving books:*[2]

Genesis (parts of Chapters 21–24), Leviticus (parts of Chapters 20–22), Numbers (parts of Chapters 5–7, 16–20 and 23–24),

[1] It is of course possible that the manuscript originally contained other books after the Shepherd of Hermas. We cannot tell. This book assumes that it did not.

[2] Details of precisely which parts survive are available on the Codex Sinaiticus Project website.

Deuteronomy (parts of Chapters 3–4 and
28–30)
Joshua (parts of Chapters 12–13), Judges
(a verse from Chapter 2 and 4.7–11.2)
1 Chronicles (parts of Chapters 17–18) and
1 Chronicles 9.27–18.19 (includes duplication
of preceding)
2 Esdras 9.9–end
Judges (missing verses in Chapters 11–13)
Lamentations (parts of Chapters 1–2)
Hermas (all of Visions, and some of
Mandates)
Complete books:
Esther, Tobit, 1 and 4 Maccabees, Isaiah,
Jeremiah
Joel, Obadiah, Jonah, Nahum, Habakkuk,
Zephaniah, Haggai, Zechariah, Malachi
Psalms, Proverbs, Ecclesiastes, Song of
Songs, Wisdom, Sirach, Job
the New Testament and Barnabas

Hermas is divided in several ways: usually, instead of having a straight chapter sequence from beginning to end, it has three sequences: Visions (5), Mandates (12) and Parables (10). Each of these sections is divided into chapters and verses. There is also a straight numbering of these chapters through the book (there are 114 of them).

REFERENCES TO PAGES IN CODEX SINAITICUS

Codex Sinaiticus does not contain page numbers. It does have two ancient systems for numbering the quires, and this book uses the older of these to navigate the manuscript. The standard quire is created (see Chapter Four) by taking **four sheets**, and folding them in half, to make **eight leaves**, known as **folios**. When the manuscript is opened flat so that two pages are visible (together they constitute an **opening**), the left hand page is called the **verso** and the right hand page the **recto**. Our indication of a page has three components:

Quire number (indicated by Q)
Folio number (indicated by F)
Recto or verso (indicated by r or v)

So the very first page of the manuscript (if it survived) would be Q1-F1r. The first page of the New Testament is Q74-F1r. No quire has more than eight folios (some have fewer). A reference without 'r' or 'v' refers to the folio, not the two pages it consists of (e.g. Q74-F1). Sometimes I also give the column number (between 1 and 4) and the line number (up to 50 or so). The first line of the manuscript would be Q1-F1r-C1-L1. The tenth line of the third column of Quire 74, Folio 1r would be Q74-F1r-C3-L10. The numbering is of the manuscript as it was originally constructed, not the manuscript as it survives today.

SOURCES AND FURTHER READING

The 'bible' for users of Codex Sinaiticus is H. J. M. Milne and T. C. Skeat, *Scribes and Correctors of the Codex Sinaiticus, including Contributions by Douglas Cockerell*, London: British Museum, 1938. Milne and Skeat also produced a summary version, *The Codex Sinaiticus and the Codex Alexandrinus*, London: British Museum, 2nd edition, 1955 (1st edition 1938).

There are two recent studies of importance: D. Jongkind, *Scribal Habits of Codex Sinaiticus* (Texts and Studies Third Series 5), Piscataway: Gorgias, 2007 and A. C. Myshrall, 'Codex Sinaiticus, its Correctors, and the Caesarean Text of the Gospels', unpublished Ph.D. thesis, University of Birmingham, 2005.

CHAPTER TWO

The Christian Book in the Age of Constantine

IN THE fourth century, Christianity became established as the dominant religion of the Roman world. Until then it had been a vigorous and expanding faith, occasionally subject to persecution. These persecutions were of different kinds. Christians received harsh treatment when they were made scapegoats by Nero for the Great Fire of Rome in 64. There are unlikely to have been direct repercussions outside the imperial capital, but the event set a precedent, and undoubtedly had a profound impact on Christian attitudes to the Roman Empire. Most persecutions were local events, traumatic for those involved but neither widespread nor long-lasting in a culture which was generally tolerant in its attitude to religious diversity. On a few occasions, however, the persecution of Christians became imperial policy, and thus far greater in degree. The most systematic and longest took place in the reign of Diocletian; it began in 303 and lasted for nine years. The destruction of their sacred writings was seen as a vital part of the elimination of Christian identity, and so the persecution began with an edict requiring the destruction of church buildings and the burning of Christian Scriptures. Further enactments permitting torture and execution of Christians were aimed at eliminating the Church's leaders.

The following exchange gives a vivid account of how Diocletian's policy was carried out. It is an official account of events in Cirta, the capital of Numidia (modern Constantine in Algeria). Cirta had had its bishop since the second century, and had seen two of them martyred in Valerian's reign fifty years earlier. First, some arrests were made. Then:

THE MAYOR: Bring out the scriptures in your possession so that we may obey the orders and commands of the emperors.

(The subdeacon Catullinus produced one very large codex)

THE MAYOR: Why have you only surrendered one codex? Produce the scriptures that you have.

THE SUBDEACONS CATULLINUS AND MARCUCLIUS: We have no more... The lectors have the codices.

[The mayor went on to visit the lectors]

(When they came to the house of Felix, the worker in marbles, he produced five codices. And when they came to the house of Victorinus, he produced eight codices. And when they came to the house of Projectus, he produced five large and two small codices. And when they came to the house of Victor the Grammarian, ... Victor produced two codices and four booklets ... And when they came to the house of Coddeo, his wife produced six codices.)

THE MAYOR: If there has been any omission, the responsibility is yours.

We cannot know how high a proportion of copies of the Scriptures was lost. But the change in Christianity's fortunes after Constantine's accession in 312 gives the surviving copies a great significance. The new emperor passed an act that 'whoever wishes to embrace this sect and religion is permitted to do so', and that churches might be built. Under not only permission, but active imperial encouragement, Christianity quickly grew in popularity, wealth and confidence. With this growth came the need for more books, besides the equally great need to replace those which had been destroyed, and so from the comparatively small gene pool of manuscripts surviving the persecution came a far larger population than there had been before. This period was therefore of great significance in the evolution of the Christian Bible. It is made even more important by the fact that until quite modern times, no copies older than this

To be more precise, 312 is the year in which Constantine became undisputed western emperor and the senior Augustus; in 324 he became the sole emperor.

Constantinian period were known. In fact, only in the nineteenth century were printed copies of the New Testament made which used manuscripts even as old as the fourth century. Even today, the two surviving major codices of the fourth century are the basis of almost all printings of the Greek Bible, and thus of translations of the New Testament into many languages. Codex Sinaiticus is one of these two. The other, Codex Vaticanus, will be described below.

And with the new-found wealth and confidence of the Constantinian age came also a dramatic change in the character of the books which Christians produced. Codex Sinaiticus is the most remarkable example of what fourth-century Christianity was able to create. To understand how new and different it would have seemed to contemporaries, we need to compare it with what had gone before, and continued to be commonplace for several further generations.

THE FORMAT OF THE CHRISTIAN BOOK

It is remarkable that earliest Christianity popularised the form of book which western culture has long taken for granted. The literary texts of Greece and Rome – Homer, Plato, Virgil – were preserved on papyrus rolls. The sacred texts of Judaism were preserved on parchment rolls. Christians copied their texts – gospels, letters, acts of apostles and apocalypses – into papyrus notebooks, made by folding sheets in half and stitching them together at the fold. They soon developed these by making a number of gatherings of sheets (quires) and stitching them together into one. The oldest surviving fragment of one of these books, a small part of a page from John's Gospel, dates from about 150. In all, around forty-seven fragments See Plate 3 of New Testament texts copied before the year 300 are known today. The largest of them is a manuscript which contained the four Gospels and Acts of the Apostles, with a page size of 25 cm high and 20 cm wide (10 × 8 in.). A more typical size is 16 × 14 cm (6 × 5½ in.). Written often in a simple style, with few embellishments and little or no aids for the reader, these were functional copies. Punctuation

Parts or most of thirty leaves survive. Papyri are rarely more than one or two.

Readers spoke out loud in antiquity, even when reading privately. The sound of the words compensated for the lack of punctuation and spaces.

was very slight (and with no spaces between words much depended upon the skill of the reader). There was nothing like the later systems of chapter and verse division. Certain particular aspects of Christian books appear very early, in particular the abbreviation of some of the most commonly occurring divine names, the principal being those for 'God', 'Christ', 'Jesus' and 'Lord'.

The fourth century sees for the first time the de luxe Christian codex. Most marked is the fact that manuscripts began to be copied on parchment as well as on papyrus, a transition which was to be complete by about 700 CE. Parchment, the skin of sheep or calf, is a stronger material than papyrus, capable of surviving in larger page sizes and being bound into more gatherings.

Written about forty years after Constantine's accession, Codex Sinaiticus reveals the extraordinary standards of technology that had already been attained. We will see later what was required in terms of parchment manufacture and book production to achieve the qualities found in the Codex. These standards are found only in one other manuscript of the era, Codex Vaticanus.

The limitations of a papyrus codex mean that the most one could have hoped to get into a single volume would be the Gospels and Acts, and this only in the largest possible format. Most of our copies of the Gospels probably only ever consisted of one of the four. The parchment codex, on the other hand, could hold far more: not merely four Gospels and Acts, but an entire copy of the oldest Christian writings, and even the entire Greek Bible. Until this technological advance, the New Testament writings could not exist as a single codex, but only as a collection of codices. The twenty-seven books of the Greek and western canon might have existed in as many as eight papyrus codices (one each for the Gospels, Acts, Catholic Epistles, Paul's letters and Revelation) or as few as three or four. The Old Testament would have consisted of many separate volumes.

Codex Sinaiticus is the most important evidence that the parchment codex physically changed the presentation of the canon of

Scripture. It became possible to copy the sacred writings in a single volume, and so to think of them as a distinct entity in the way in which we do today. Such a collection can give the writings a sense of being different, by presenting them in a uniform manner, with features not used in copying other works.

It seems surprising that Greek-speaking Christianity showed only brief interest in the idea of a one-volume Bible. There are four surviving ancient Greek Bibles, and three later ones (all from the fourteenth to fifteenth centuries). Even one-volume copies of one testament on its own are a rarity: for the New Testament there are sixty-one, all of them copied after the year 900.

By contrast, a complete Bible was less unusual in the Latin-speaking western world from the ninth-century Renaissance onwards. From even earlier, we know that single-volume editions of the Bible were being produced in Italy in the second half of the sixth century. In the early eighth, three great Bibles were produced in the monastery of Monkwearmouth-Jarrow, in the north-east of England.

The same situation applied at the invention of printing. Gutenberg produced a complete Bible in Latin straight away. But it was to be nearly another seventy years before the entire Greek New Testament saw the light of day, with the entire Greek Bible coming a little later. The one-volume Bible is a product of the Latin part of the Christian heritage. But it may be traced back to Codex Sinaiticus through the ancient Latin tradition.

Since reference has just been made to *four* ancient Greek Bibles, it is clear that Codex Sinaiticus does not stand quite alone. It is time to introduce three other manuscripts.

The most important of these is Codex Vaticanus, a manuscript in the Vatican Library. It was produced at about the same time as Codex Sinaiticus. In fact some authorities believe it to be slightly older. It breaks off in the letter to the Hebrews, which is why Codex Sinaiticus' claim to be the oldest complete New Testament is unchallenged. Its appearance is almost as magnificent, but it is slightly

As of 29 September 2008, there were 5,555 manuscripts in the register of Greek New Testament manuscripts. Nobody has a precise figure for the Greek Old Testament, but it is less than half as many.

One of these, Codex Amiatinus, was sent to Italy as a present to the pope and is today in Florence.

smaller, and has only three columns to the page. The two manuscripts are very similar in their wording of the New Testament. In the Old Testament, they sometimes support different versions of the text. Where they differ in the New Testament, most editors believe that the text of Codex Vaticanus is generally more reliable than that of Codex Sinaiticus. But as a book it comes second. This is not only because of its smaller format. At some point in the Middle Ages, its fading ink was written over, so that the original characters are obscured.

The other two manuscripts were written in the fifth century. Codex Alexandrinus (its name associates it with the Patriarch of Alexandria, who gave it to Charles I in 1627) is another manuscript in the British Library. In fact it usually shares a showcase with Codex Sinaiticus. In many books of the Bible editors regard it as a useful guide to the oldest form of the text. Codex Ephraemi Rescriptus means 'The rewritten codex of Ephrem'. In the twelfth century, it was taken apart and its parchment scraped and turned through ninety degrees into a new page size to take a text by Ephrem the Syrian. As a result of this, it is lacking much of the text. Where it is available (in parts of the wisdom books, and much of the New Testament), it is sometimes a very valuable witness, notably in the Apocalypse.

Ephrem (*c.* 307–73) was the greatest Syrian poet and theologian. His works were also very influential in their Greek translations.

These three fine manuscripts are among the most important copies of the Bible. But they are none of them as impressive as Codex Sinaiticus, with its page size of 43 × 38 cm. Only one other Greek New Testament manuscript is taller, and none are wider. These dimensions give a page area of 0.1634 m². The manuscript which seems most like it, Codex Vaticanus, with a page size of 27 × 27 cm, has a page area of only 0.0729 m².

The breadth of the whole opening is 76 cm. This far exceeds the size of Codex Vaticanus and Ephraemi Rescriptus (54 cm when open) and of Alexandrinus (52 cm). The Latin Codex Amiatinus with a height of 48.9 cm and an opening of 68 cm wide comes closer. The format of four columns to a page is unique for Greek and Latin manuscripts. The entire opening, with eight columns, has the appearance of a roll, although a roll would not need to be unrolled so wide for ordinary reading purposes.

CONSTANTINE AND CODEX SINAITICUS

It is clear how significant Constantine's policies were for the history of Christianity, and consequently for the development of the book. They made the conditions in which Codex Sinaiticus was created. It is interesting then to find that it has been claimed that the Codex may even have been written at the emperor's express command. The reason for this is a passage in Eusebius' *Life of Constantine*, where he reproduces a letter which he had received on the topic of copying the Scriptures:

Victor Constantinus Maximus Augustus to Eusebius.

In the city named after us [Constantinople] a great crowd of people have, thanks to the providence of the Saviour God, devoted themselves to the most holy Church. Since everything in the city is growing so quickly, it is obviously appropriate to build more churches. Be prepared to act at once on our decision. We make known to you that you are to commission fifty volumes which are to be bound in leather, easy to read and (for convenience) portable. They are to be written by craftsmen who are both calligraphers and used to working accurately. They are to be copies of the divine Scriptures, which you well know must be available for reading in church. We have sent written word to the Financial Director of the Diocese, who is to ensure that all necessary materials are provided. So that the written volumes may be prepared very quickly, let this work receive your attention. Moreover by the authority of this our letter you receive the power to requisition two public vehicles to transport them. These are the best means by which the books may be written calligraphically and easily dispatched for our inspection of them. Of course this will be carried out by one of the deacons of your church, who when he comes will experience our generosity.

May God watch over you, dear brother.

Eusebius' name frequently occurs in discussions of Codex Sinaiticus. He was Bishop of Caesarea, dying in 340. One of the leading writers of his age, he wrote a *History of the Church* which is one of our most important sources for the study of early Christianity.

The Diocese was one of the units of the empire created in Diocletian's administrative reform.

Presumably the deacon's task was to ensure the safe arrival of the copies.

Eusebius continues:

Thus the emperor instructed. Action immediately followed word, as we sent him threes and fours in curiously worked bindings.

At first sight this appears clear, and certain similarities with Codex Sinaiticus and Codex Vaticanus may occur to one, for example that these de luxe complete Bibles are so impressive that they might be the product of imperial patronage, and that Eusebius' reference to producing them 'in threes and fours' might refer to the layouts of the manuscripts which he had made (namely the three columns to a page of Codex Vaticanus and four of Codex Sinaiticus). The argument that two of the fifty survive carries with it two assumptions about an imperial production: that the quality will have been superior; and that their preservation is due in part to the added prestige of such a book.

But when we begin to look at this story in more detail, difficulties with the letter and with identifying any extant manuscript as one of the fifty begin to emerge. In fact, the more we study it, the less certain we can be about what was intended. In the first place, it is often said that Constantine ordered fifty Bibles for fifty churches in Constantinople. The wording does not necessarily mean that the copies were complete Bibles. I have translated the phrase as 'divine Scriptures'. The assumption that each copy contained the entire Greek Bible may owe more to modern familiarity with printed Bibles, which normally contain both testaments, each in its entirety. But it has already been argued that complete copies such as Codex Sinaiticus were a rarity in the ancient world.

One's suspicion that the story is not straightforward may grow when one discovers that the successful expansion of the Church in Constantinople is unlikely to have been such that fifty new churches were built. It has been suggested that in the entire empire there are only twenty-three church buildings which 'may with reasonable confidence be attributed to Constantine as patron or founder, together with several others which may be considered live possibilities'. Of these, five were built in the new capital: Hagia Eirene, Hagia Sophia, St Acacius in Heptascalon, the Archangel Michael at Anaplus (all started after 326) and the Church of the Holy Apostles and Mausoleum of Constantine (after 330). Another five churches are attributed to the Constantinian dynasty, and at the very least have a fourth-century date. Of these, it has been suggested that one (St Mocius) was also built by Constantine. Even if the numbers are approximate, they fall far short of the fifty buildings, each requiring a complete Bible, necessary for the standard interpretation of the passage. Nor should we accept uncritically the claim that imperial patronage indicated superior workmanship. The pagan historian Zosimus (whose account of Constantine provides a good antidote to Eusebius' hagiography) records that he 'expended the public treasure in unnecessary and unprofitable buildings' and 'built some which soon after were taken down again, because they were built too quickly and did not stand up'. Contrast this with Eusebius' account of the emperor's church-building programme in his capital (3.47).

Zosimus' New History was written in the period 590–610.

What can be learned about the manuscripts commissioned from Eusebius? Clearly, the fact of the commissioning is in itself significant, along with the instruction that the materials and the transportation of the finished product were to be supplied from public funds. The instructions about the books suggest that the interest is in useful rather than in impressive books: they are to have leather bindings (for durability), to be easily legible, and to be portable. The requirement that they should be made by skilled scribes and written well does not necessarily indicate that they should be beautiful, as some translate the penultimate sentence of the letter. That is to say, calligraphy refers to good professional rather than second-class work, in which beauty is secondary to the pragmatic awareness that such products may have represented better value for money.

Another difficulty with interpreting the passage is that there seems to be something missing from the text of Eusebius after the sentence referring to threes and fours (or so editors have suspected). In fact the translation 'threes and fours' is doubtful.

I suppose that if one took together the possibility that each of the fifty manuscripts contained a part of the Scriptures, and took an approximation of ten churches requiring copies, one could easily suppose that each church could require five manuscripts: for example, a Pentateuch, a Psalter, the Prophets, the Gospels and Paul's letters. This is not an impossible way of treating Eusebius' account as accurate. But any connection with Codex Sinaiticus is thereby denied.

Another argument against identifying Codex Sinaiticus as one of the fifty is that it is generally considered to have been written in the period 350–60, one or two decades after Constantine's death in 337.

In any case, Constantine was not the only emperor to commission Bibles. In about 341, the Patriarch Athanasius of Alexandria[1] provided the Emperor Constans with a number of copies:

I sent to him bound volumes of the holy Scriptures, which he had ordered me to prepare for him.[2]

At that time, Athanasius was in exile in Rome, from where Constans was ruling. Assuming (very reasonably) that these were Greek copies, Codex Sinaiticus is as plausibly one of these copies as one of the set made for Constantine.

But how many other manuscripts were written for how many other imperial patrons, under circumstances about which we now know nothing? And how many for wealthy patrons who were not emperors? The answer has to be that to try to tidy up history so neatly, with Codex Sinaiticus the result of an independently attested event, is over-confident by far. The commissions by Constantine and by Constans are examples of one way in which a manuscript such as Codex Sinaiticus might have been made. But we can say no more than that.

[1] He was bishop from 328 till his death in 373 (with frequent periods of exile, which is why he became known as 'Athanasius against the world').

[2] This passage is not so well known as the letter to Eusebius, perhaps because of the view first suggested by J. A. Fabricius (1668–1736) that Athanasius gave the emperor a copy of *A Synopsis of Sacred Scripture*, a summary of the biblical books. But this work is now known not to have been written by Athanasius.

SOURCES AND FURTHER READING

The account of the search for books at the beginning of the chapter is from the *Gesta apud Zenophilum*, the report of the trial of a group in Numidia. It is preserved in a work on the issue of apostasy, written by the North African writer Optatus in about 385–90, *Against Parmenianus the Donatist*. The full text is available online at http://www.tertullian.org/fathers/optatus_10_appendix2.htm (the first appendix is a document from the same period in which codices again play an important part). See further H. Y. Gamble, *Books and Readers in the Early Church. A History of Early Christian Texts*, New Haven and London: Yale University Press, 1995, pp. 144ff. This work is a valuable study of early Christian book culture.

I have made my own translation of Eusebius' *Life of Constantine*, using the edition by F. Winkelmann, *Eusebius Werke*, Part 1, Vol. 1 (*Die griechischen christlichen Schriftsteller der ersten Jahrhunderte*), 2nd edition, Berlin: Akademie-Verlag, 1975. The passage may be found in Book 4, Chapter 36.

For the composition of the *Life of Constantine*, see H. A. Drake, 'What Eusebius Knew: The Genesis of the "Vita Constantini"', *Classical Philology* 83 (1988), pp. 20–38.

Athanasius' *Apology to Constantius* (the quotation is from Chapter 4) is available online at http://www.ccel.org/ccel/schaff/npnf204

I found my suspicions about Constantine's fifty copies supported by G. A. Robbins, '"Fifty Copies of the Sacred Writings" (*Vigiliae Christianae* 4.36): Entire Bibles or Gospel Books?', in E. A. Livingstone (ed.), *Studia Patristica Vol. XIX. Papers Presented to the Tenth International Conference of Patristic Studies Held in Oxford 1987. Historica, Theologica, Gnostica, Biblica et Apocrypha*, Leuven: Peeters, 1989, pp. 91–98.

For imperial church-building, I am indebted to G. T. Armstrong, 'Constantine's Churches', *Gesta* 6 (1967), pp. 1–9 and M. J. Johnson, 'Architecture of Empire', in N. Lenski (ed.), *The Cambridge Companion to the Age of Constantine*, New York: Cambridge University Press, 2006, pp. 278–97, esp. p. 292. The quotation from Zosimus is taken from Book 2.

A lavishly illustrated and informative book about the older history of the Bible is M. P. Brown (ed.), *In the Beginning. Bibles Before the Year 1000*, Washington D.C.: Smithsonian Institution, 2006. Even more sumptuous is

C. de Hamel, *The Book. A History of the Bible*, London and New York: Phaidon, 2001, which spans the origins to the present day.

Codex Alexandrinus is discussed by Scot McKendrick, 'The Codex Alexandrinus or The Dangers of Being a Named Manuscript', in S. McKendrick and O. A. O'Sullivan (eds), *The Bible as Book. The Transmission of the Greek Text*, London: British Library and New Castle, Del.: Oak Knoll Press, 2003, pp. 1–16.

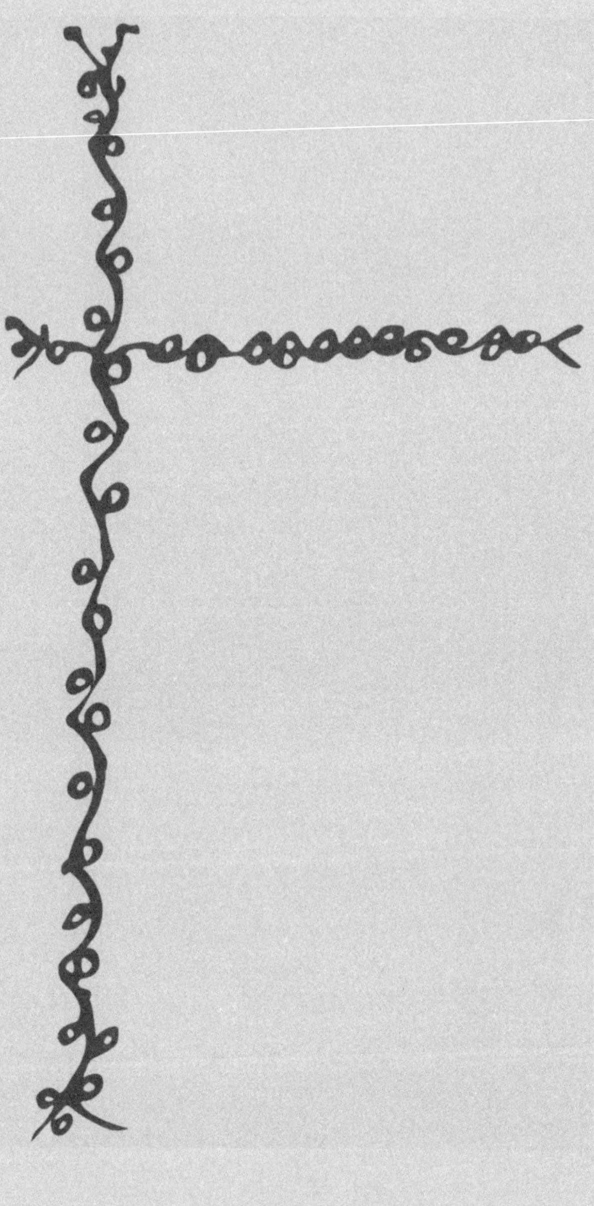

CHAPTER THREE

Making a Bible in the Year 350

CRIBES were not like typists or typesetters. The fact that they could control the exact shape of every mark they made gave them a much greater freedom, so that they should be considered as artists. They could produce attractive left margins by taking into account the different letter shapes, they could write smaller letters at a line's end, they could even write several letters with strokes in common. Other materials such as headings, marginal text and chapter numbers could be written in a different script and size, and their exact position on the page could be controlled. The result in the hands of an expert scribe was a clearly legible page with a fluid beauty quite different from anything in printed or digital format.

Another defining characteristic of the manuscript book is the process of correction, both at the time of its production and subsequently. In the making of a printed book, the type is set up and printed out as proofs, so that the type may be corrected until it is satisfactory. The closest that the production of Codex Sinaiticus comes to the modern situation is with several 'cancel leaves', where a different scribe has written replacement pages within a block written by one of the others. This apart, a manuscript book could only be improved by corrections which are obviously corrections. In a well-produced manuscript, a process of correction was carried out before it left the hands of the scribes. Certainly these were made neatly, but unless the scribe was able to wash off the ink before it had

One may also observe places where a scribe began to write the wrong letter, and then adjusted the strokes to complete the right one, so that for example a curve has been disguised as a vertical stroke.

See Plates 3a and 3b

A particularly complicated example of some correcting is discussed in Chapter Six, pp. 87–89.

These will be explained in more detail in Chapter Seven.

dried, some trace of what was first written will always remain. Corrections made by subsequent users also relate to the original text in a different way from those in a printed book. Manuscript annotations in a modern book are obviously different from the printed text. But in a manuscript everything is written by hand. Looking at a page of Codex Sinaiticus, the different layers of correction intermingle. The issue is clear from certain features of the transcription made by the Project. The transcription generally gives the text as it was first written by the scribe. But sometimes, where the scribe's first version of the text has been erased and is no longer legible, we have presented the text as it was corrected by one of the original production team. In a few other places, there is a block of text which is such a striking part of the page that it is included in the margin of the transcription. See for example the bottom of Q35-F4v-C4, where an explanation is visible, or the top of Q36-F5v-C3, where some text (for Esther 1.5) has been supplied in the top margin by the same corrector. Such changes have permanently altered the appearance of the manuscript.

A third difference between a manuscript and a printed book lies in the unique character of the text of every manuscript copy of a writing. Each scribe produced a different wording of the text being copied. The kind of changes that will have occurred range from alterations in the spelling which reflect the way the scribe was used to speaking the word rather than the correct spelling, through a wide range of unconscious errors, to places where conscious decisions were made. What is important to note here is that as part of the copying process scribes will have had to deal with difficulties which they noticed in the manuscript from which they were copying (known as the exemplar). While these should have been picked up at a preparatory stage, it is reasonable to assume that there must have been occasions when copyists found a difficulty in the exemplar after they had already written part of the problematical text, and decided it was easier to make adjustments to the next words to be copied.

28

The peculiarities of copying by hand as opposed to printing apply to all texts. What follows applies specifically to the Bible. Again, the differences from the modern world, of which two should be singled out, are striking. Today, Christian denominations specify which books in their judgement belong to the Bible. They may even have particular authoritative versions of them (although these may not be the ones which people actually use). In the fourth century, argument with regard to the books to be treated as canonical was still at a formative stage, and there was certainly no concept of a single authoritative form of text of each book. The second difference was discussed in Chapter Two: that before the middle of the fourth century, there was no concept of the Bible as the result of a single production process. What were available were copies of parts of the Bible, for example the Minor Prophets, a Gospel, or the letters of Paul. For both these reasons, the biggest challenge to the producers of Codex Sinaiticus was to decide which books were to be included.

CHOOSING THE BOOKS

Codex Sinaiticus contains, from a modern western point of view, four categories of text:

the Old Testament books of the Hebrew Scriptures
the additional Old Testament books of the Greek Scriptures
the New Testament
two other early Christian writings

The New Testament is the most straightforward of these sets of texts, so it will be described first.

The New Testament

The New Testament as it is found in Codex Sinaiticus contains the twenty-seven books treated as canonical by the majority of denominations. This list is first prescribed in a document written in 367. Some background is necessary to explain this. The date of

Some Eastern Orthodox denominations do not accept what are called the Minor Catholic Epistles, namely 2 and 3 John, 2 Peter and Jude, so that they have a canon of twenty-three books.

Easter, then as now, is determined by the interrelationships of the solar and lunar calendars, and this date determines the rest of the church's year. While these may today be determined very quickly for any year, either past or future, in late antiquity the decision required expertise, and was announced each year. Alexandria had been renowned for astronomical research for centuries. In the third century BCE, Eratosthenes produced a fairly accurate calculation of the earth's circumference and invented the leap day; two hundred years later, Sosigenes is said to have advised Julius Caesar on his reformed calendar. Christianity came to draw on this expertise to find the date of Easter each year. By the middle of the third century, the Bishop of Alexandria would send out a letter at Epiphany, announcing the date of Easter. The oldest known letters were by Dionysius, who was bishop from 248 to about 264. By the middle of the fourth century, a system had developed whereby the Bishop of Alexandria would communicate the correct date to his fellow-bishops in Rome and Antioch, who would then each distribute the message in his half of the Christian world. This annual festal letter represented an opportunity to communicate other kinds of information as well, and the opportunity was fully used by Athanasius. His Thirty-ninth Festal Letter of 367 sets out what he regards as the canonical books.

Athanasius' letter does not survive directly. It has been reconstructed from quotations, in Greek and in other languages.

A catechumen is a candidate for baptism.

It is often said that a canonical list has the purpose not so much of including certain books as of *excluding* others. But it is not so simple as that, and Athanasius' letter shows why. In both his Old and his New Testament list, he discriminates between canonical books and books which are to be used for the instruction of catechumens. This second category includes one extremely popular early Christian text, namely the Shepherd of Hermas. So he did not disapprove of this book. In fact, elsewhere he describes it as divinely inspired. It seems that for Athanasius a writing could be part of Scripture and yet not be canonical. We have to be careful about imposing later categories which distinguish between divinely inspired and canonical books on the one hand (which are found in the Bible), and all other writings on the other (which are not contained in the Bible).

This information helps us to understand why Codex Sinaiticus contains the Shepherd of Hermas and another early Christian writing not mentioned by Athanasius, the Epistle of Barnabas. First, a brief description of each:

The Shepherd of Hermas seems to have been a very popular text, for many fragments of old papyrus copies have been found in Egypt. Probably written in the middle of the second century in Rome, it is an apocalyptic work in the vein of Revelation, dealing with important issues of the day. The author's identity is unknown.[1]

In spite of its claim to be by Barnabas the companion of Paul, the Epistle of Barnabas is a text by an unknown author, who was probably an Alexandrian, writing at some point between the destruction of Jerusalem in 70 and its rebuilding under Hadrian after 135. It deals with the Old Testament, using allegory to assert the truth of the Christian interpretation of its meaning.

People have sometimes been puzzled by the presence of these two texts within the pages of the Codex. This is because it is easy to assume that because Codex Sinaiticus is a Bible, it must therefore, like our Bibles, contain only canonical books. But if we remember how for Athanasius books could be inspired yet not canonical, it becomes clear that the makers of the manuscript (not just the scribes, but probably the person or persons who commissioned it) had a wider concept of using the potential of the parchment codex to include a wide selection of inspired books, not just those which were emerging as canonical.

The Old Testament[2]

There is a similar situation with regard to the Old Testament books, even though it is more complicated.[3]

Christianity has never been able to agree whether to adopt the more restricted canon of the Hebrew Scriptures books, or the larger canon of the Greek Septuagint. The differences between the two consist not only of the selection of books and their order, but also

[1] Hermas receives oracles from an angel who takes the guise of a shepherd.

[2] The title 'Old Testament' is a Christian name for a collection of pre-Christian texts. The origins of the terminology rest with the North African Latin Christian Tertullian, writing in around 200. It is most convenient to use in the context of discussing this Christian codex.

[3] The Hebrew Scriptures were only studied by a few Christian scholars, notably Origen (who will appear more than once below) and Jerome, whose translation of the Hebrew Scriptures into Latin became the definitive western version.

of thousands of differences in the text, some of them being very significant for its meaning. These will be described separately (see pp. 93–100). But before their respective contents are described, it is necessary to refer briefly to the origins of each.

The Hebrew writings came into being through more or less complicated processes that include oral tradition and early written forms which were then combined and revised once or several times. Some make reference to lost writings such as the Annals of the Kings of Judah, mentioned in the Books of Kings. Some, such as Jonah, have apparently a simpler composition history. Some are difficult to date accurately, while others developed over a long period. Isaiah, for example, represents a long tradition of prophetic activity and not the work of a single individual. These books are variously myth, legend, prophetic tradition, poetry, drama, fiction, historical narrative, legal code, wisdom literature. What is important to remember is that their composition does not correspond to the modern authorial process with which we are familiar. In this, an individual writes a text, which is sent to a publisher who makes multiple identical copies, which are then distributed and sold. There is a very strong emphasis on the individual author, because the publication process controls the content of the book. To apply this cult of the author to the ancient world is anachronistic. A better analogy for many of the books of the Old Testament may be the process of compilation of a Wikipedia article. The article grows through the changes and additions made by a series of contributors, and the more an article is used the more likely it is to be changed. There is no point (yet, at any rate) at which the article reaches a final form, and any copies of it stored in individual computers will represent stages which may or may not correspond to the versions stored in other computers. If we apply this model to the process of creation of the Old Testament writings, it will be seen that major differences between ancient written copies are likely to represent different stages of composition and revision. In fact, we do not have copies which are old enough to establish many of the details of this process of growth. But the copies which we do have, including Codex Sinaiticus, provide evidence that there was such a process.

This process of growth is very different from modern book production in another way. An author will write and write, producing drafts, revising and refining. These stages are hidden from the reader, because the author sends the publisher a single definitive version from which the distributed text is made. But without the single publishing stage, the distinction between composition and distribution is weakened. Different forms and stages of text will have been in circulation.

There is yet another reason why the stages at which these texts came into a literary form which we would recognise is often hard to determine. The oldest complete copy of the Hebrew Scriptures (the Leningrad Codex), on which the commonly used modern translations depend, is very recent, having been copied in 1008. The Leningrad Codex represents the Massoretic Text. This is an extremely thorough edition of the text which was developed in the early medieval period, which sought to retain the form known to its editors even in places where it was obscure or without evident meaning, along with a very extensive system of notes called the Massorah. It has only been since the discovery of the Dead Sea Scrolls fifty years ago that scholarship has been able to ascertain what had been suspected by some, namely that even in the first century of the Common Era the Hebrew Scriptures also circulated in copies containing significant differences from the Leningrad Codex. It is now generally acknowledged that up to this time and beyond at least some of the writings existed in at least two divergent forms. Until the Dead Sea discoveries, the principal evidence for the existence of these divergent forms had been the ancient Greek version known as the Septuagint.

THE SEPTUAGINT

According to an ancient tradition, the Pharaoh Ptolemy Philadelphus (ruled 283–246 BCE) wished his library at Alexandria to contain a copy of every book in the world. Through the mediation of Aristeas, the supposed author of the work in which this tradition is recounted, seventy-two devout old men versed in the Law, six from each of the twelve tribes of Israel, were selected to translate the Jewish Law into Greek. They were brought from Judah to Alexandria, and after a feast lasting seven days, were set on an island where they could work in peace. At the end of seventy-two days they completed their translation. In a later account, the Alexandrian Jewish philosopher Philo (20 BCE–50 CE) writes that each of the seventy translators independently produced exactly the same translation as all the others.

The reality is less simple and more prosaic. Detailed analysis of the translation technique of the different books of the Septuagint has led to the conclusion that the Septuagint is the sum of a number of separate translations, arising out of the same cultural milieu, namely the Jewish diaspora in Egypt, and particularly in Alexandria. There is thus at least one germ of historical reality in Aristeas' story. This diaspora had its origins in the Babylonian Exile, the deportation of many Jews to Babylon after the capture of Jerusalem by Nebuchadnezzar in 586 BCE. But the principal event which gave Alexandria a large and flourishing Jewish quarter was the fact that when Alexander the Great founded the city in 332 BCE he encouraged Jews to settle there. Alexandria may have been in Egypt, but it was a Greek city. Increasingly, the Jews of Alexandria became Greek-speaking to the point where a translation into the language became inevitable. The resultant version is the most influential of all the translations of the Bible.

Because there was no point in antiquity at which the Hebrew texts became fixed, the Septuagint is important for two reasons. In the first place, it provides evidence for the wording of the Hebrew copies from which the translation was made. These copies were much older than any copies surviving today. The Septuagint is therefore important in understanding what the texts were like in the third to first centuries BCE.

But not all the differences between the Septuagint and the Hebrew copies reflect differences between ancient and later Hebrew copies. Some reflect the second way in which the Septuagint is important, namely as evidence for the changing interpretation of the text. Of course a translation always betrays the translator's understanding of the text. But the Septuagint also contains thousands of significant changes, some of which are expansions, abbreviations or rearrangements, as well as a different canon of books, and many details throughout the text.

It is important to bear in mind that while the Septuagint as a *translation* was produced in the third century BCE, the *copies* which we have are not so old. A fourth-century CE copy such as Codex Sinaiticus will not always represent accurately the intentions of a translator of the book of Genesis, working five hundred years earlier. We can only access the Hebrew writing by means of the later copies, and we can only access the Septuagint by means of the later copies. That is all that we possess. That this is a serious issue may best be seen when the later history of the Septuagint, and of other Greek versions of the Bible, is understood.

History of the Greek versions

The Septuagint began as a translation of the Five Books of Moses (Genesis, Exodus, Leviticus, Numbers and Deuteronomy). The process of translating all the books which were to become a part of the Septuagint lasted four centuries, so that it was only in the first century of the Common Era that all of them were available.

The Septuagint was not the only Greek translation to be made in antiquity. Six others are known from the great edition of the Greek Old Testament by the third-century Christian Alexandrian scholar Origen, the Hexapla (see below). Modern research has also found more than one version of the Septuagint text of some books.

It would again be anachronistic to attribute to these different versions a fixed and unchanging wording. Today it is generally considered more accurate to regard them all together as products of a continuing process of change to a broad stream of copies of the Greek Bible. In fact one might say that the process of change, coupled with the inevitable textual variation which arises in the copying of texts by hand, leads to something better described as rich soup than as a stream. Codex Sinaiticus is an important witness to this process, in the form of text copied by the production team, and in many of the corrections made by the subsequent correctors.

Origen and his Hexapla

Of particular interest is the place of Origen in the history of the Septuagint, and its relationship to Codex Sinaiticus. Origen (c. 185–c. 254) was both one of the most significant thinkers of early Christianity, and one of its greatest scholars. His most remarkable achievement in this regard was his edition of the Septuagint known as the Hexapla, because it had six columns. It is generally supposed that only one complete copy ever existed. This copy was kept in the library at Caesarea and was known to Eusebius. The columns contained the Hebrew text, a transliteration of it, and the different Greek versions (some of which are simply named after the column number). The original was lost long ago. What survives are a few fragments of partial copies, marginal notes in manuscripts in Greek and evidence from a Syriac version. The Hexapla is of particular interest for the study of Codex Sinaiticus, since a link with it is claimed by one of the correctors of Codex Sinaiticus (see Chapter Six).

Comparing the Hebrew Bible and the Septuagint

The Hebrew Bible is divided into three parts: the Law, the Prophets and the Writings. It consists of the following thirty-nine books (in the order of the Massoretic Text):

The Law	Genesis, Exodus, Leviticus, Numbers, Deuteronomy
The Prophets	Joshua, Judges, 1 and 2 Samuel, 1 and 2 Kings, Isaiah, Jeremiah, Ezekiel, the Twelve

	Prophets (Hosea, Joel, Amos, Obadiah, Jonah, Micah, Nahum, Habakkuk, Zephaniah, Haggai, Zechariah, Malachi)
The Writings	Psalms, Job, Proverbs, Ruth, Canticles, Ecclesiastes, Lamentations, Esther, Daniel, Ezra, Nehemiah, 1 and 2 Chronicles

Of these, some portions were written in Aramaic, namely Daniel 2.4b–7.28 and Ezra.

The second and third groups contain several subdivisions, which although possibly later than the fourth century CE in origin, will be convenient to use. In the Prophets these are:

Former Prophets	Joshua, Judges and the books of Samuel and Kings
Latter Prophets	Isaiah, Jeremiah, Ezekiel, the Twelve Prophets (in English often called the Minor Prophets)

Within the Writings, Ruth, Canticles, Ecclesiastes, Lamentations and Esther form a group known as the Five Scrolls, while Ezra, Nehemiah and Chronicles were originally a single work.

This is the place to mention two other differences between the Hebrew and Greek texts.

1 Esdras is a work not found in the Hebrew, being taken (with additions) from the end of 2 Chronicles, Ezra and the beginning of Nehemiah.

Ezra and Nehemiah are treated as a single work, and called 2 Esdras, Nehemiah being Chapter Eleven to the end.

This 2 Esdras is not the 2 Esdras found in the English Apocrypha, which is a translation from Latin of a lost Greek book. Hence you will find the 2 Esdras of the Septuagint is sometimes called 4 Esdras (and the Septuagint 1 Esdras is sometimes called 3 Esdras). This is confusing. What matters for present purposes is that 1 Esdras and 2 Esdras refer to the *Septuagint*'s 1 Esdras and 2 Esdras.

The reason for the confusion lies in the Latin tradition.

The Septuagint has a quite different construction than the Hebrew canon and contains more books. Cyril, Patriarch of

Jerusalem from about 349 to his death in 387, gave his catechumens the following instruction, which he evidently believed would help them to learn the names of the books by heart:

Read the Holy Scriptures, these two and twenty books of the Old Testament, which were interpreted by the seventy-two interpreters . . . ; and these, if thou art diligent, strive to remember by name, as I repeat them. Of the Law, are the first five books of Moses; Genesis, Exodus, Leviticus, Numbers, Deuteronomy: then Joshua the son of Nun; and the books of Judges and of Ruth, which is numbered the seventh. Of the remaining Historical books, the first and second books of Kingdoms are among the Hebrews one book, and so the third and fourth books; and likewise the first and second books of Chronicles make one book; and the first and second books of Esdras are one; and the twelfth is the book of Esther: these are the Historical books. The books which are written in verse are five; Job, and the book of Psalms, and Proverbs, and Ecclesiastes, and the Song of Songs, which is the seventeenth book. After these come the five prophetic books: the one book of the Twelve Prophets; the book of Isaiah; the book of Jeremiah, which with Baruch, the Lamentations and the Epistle makes one book; then Ezekiel; and the book of Daniel is the twenty-second book of the Old Testament.

The Epistle of Jeremiah is a Greek letter condemning idol worship addressed to the Jews in exile in Babylon. For Baruch, see Jeremiah Chapter 36.

Athanasius accepts these twenty-two books. In fact the number twenty-two is itself symbolic, corresponding to the twenty-two letters of the Hebrew alphabet. But he also lists a number of books which again are suitable for use, even though they are not canonical. And in fact they too are part of the Septuagint, so that the twenty-two books of Cyril and Athanasius are the same as are found in the Hebrew canon (except for Baruch and the Epistle of Jeremiah, which are not in it, but seem to be included by virtue of their association with Jeremiah). So while they both speak of the Septuagint as the Christian Old Testament, they only give canonical status to the books which are also in the Hebrew canon, but follow the order of the Septuagint.

The other books present in the Septuagint but not the shorter Hebrew canon are:

The Wisdom of Solomon
The Wisdom of Sirach, known in English as Ecclesiasticus
Judith
Tobit
added portions of Daniel
four books of the Maccabees

Additions to Daniel include Bel and the Dragon, Susannah, and the Song of the Three (also known as the Benedicite).

These are listed by Athanasius as suitable to be read to catechumens.

Such is the Septuagint, and such its relationship to the Hebrew Bible. The two collections of text remain significant for Christianity. The Greek Orthodox recognise the Septuagint as their Old Testament, while western Protestant denominations generally accept the Hebrew Bible as authoritative. Roman Catholicism, since the discussion of the matter by the Council of Trent in 1548, has accepted the canonicity of all books of the Septuagint except for 1 and 2 Esdras. Anglicanism has taken a stance similar to that of Athanasius, following the injunction that the books only in the Septuagint are valuable 'for example of life and instruction of manners'.

CONCLUSION

Codex Sinaiticus therefore contains both canonical books and books suitable to be read for the edification of catechumens. It should be remembered that at this time the unbaptised were not permitted to be present at acts of worship. Thus, the context of Codex Sinaiticus is not so narrow as the liturgy, but belongs within a wider sphere as a collection of edifying books. Does this suggest anything with regard to the purpose of the manuscript? The inclusion of books not read in the liturgy suggests that it was not designed (as we might say) for the lectern, or at any rate solely for the lectern. Was it intended for wider use in a church community? Was it for the use of an individual or a family or a community? All these suggestions are possible.

Given the uncertainties which have been highlighted in this description, especially with regard to the Old Testament portions, one may appreciate that the compilers of the Codex had a series of decisions to make about what to include. They also had to work out an order for the books. Not everything went smoothly, as we will discover. We are reminded again that they were using a new technology to develop a new concept. Some of their struggles will become clear in the next three chapters.

SOURCES AND FURTHER READING

The quotation from Cyril is slightly adapted from John Henry Newman's translation: *The Catechetical Lectures of S. Cyril*, Oxford: Parker and London: Rivington, 1845, Lecture IV, Paragraphs 33 and 35 (pp. 49 and 50).

For translations of the Shepherd of Hermas and Barnabas, alongside the Greek text, see M. W. Holmes, *The Apostolic Fathers. Greek Texts and English Translations*, Grand Rapids, Mich.: Baker Books, 2007.

For a general introduction to the Septuagint, see J. M. Dines, ed. M. A. Knibb, *The Septuagint*, London and New York: Continuum, 2004.

The Anglican formulary is contained in The Thirty-Nine Articles of 1563, Article 6.

CHAPTER FOUR

Setting to Work

W HAT are the components of a manuscript book? Parchment, ink and binding material. How were these raw materials combined? The parchment was prepared and folded, the ink was made, the text was written out with a reed pen and the sheets were bound together at the folds with protective material covering the front, spine and back. What was the role of the scribes? To complete or to oversee all these stages.

Scribes are associated in our minds with the writing out of texts. But, especially when they were working as a team in making so large and unusual a book as Codex Sinaiticus, the task was much more complex. Certainly the copying of the text is the *raison d'être* of the whole enterprise, but for much of the time the scribes will also have been preoccupied with the number of sheets of parchment needing to be prepared, whether the ink was running out, how to plan their time, and how to get the text onto the page.

THE PARCHMENT

It is not surprising that the skins most often used to make parchment come from two of the most common domestic animals, namely cattle and sheep. It will be remembered that parchment came into regular use for making books in the course of the fourth century. It is distinguished from leather by the fact that it is not tanned. The purpose of the manufacturing process was to remove hair from the outside of the skin and grease from the inside, and to produce a

'Dog dung contains pancreatic enzymes which were used in solution to attack the non-collagenous proteins in skins or hides' (British School of Leather Technology, Issue 2358 of *New Scientist* magazine, 31 August 2002, p. 27).

smooth writing material of the desired thickness. No doubt the details and order of the process varied in different manufactories, but what follows is a possible sequence. First of all the skin was roughly scraped down. Then it was soaked in a bath in a process known as puring. There were two ways of doing this. In the one the bath was alkaline in character, containing lime; in the other it was acid, the active component being dog dung. Analysis of Codex Sinaiticus in the course of the Project has encouraged the theory that the parchment may have been prepared by the acid bath process. The skin was then removed from the bath, and the hair and fat scraped off. Next it was returned to the bath for further soaking, and then washed out, stretched and scraped thinner while wet. After drying out, it was scraped to its final thinness, cut to size, and pounced (rubbed down) with pumice stone.

Sometimes the whorls made by the pumice stone are visible. Several different patterns appear in Codex Sinaiticus, but it would be going beyond the current evidence to claim that this is because each scribe favoured a particular motion.

Tischendorf advanced the romantic notion that the parchment might be antelope hide. But there are places where traces of hair follicles are visible, and examination of the entry point of the hair into the skin through a microscope reveals that some sheets are cattle hide and some are sheep skin. The extraordinarily fine quality of the former suggests that it is uterine. Although the strict meaning of the term uterine suggests that it is the skin of unborn calves, in practice it includes that of young beasts. The size of the sheets of Codex Sinaiticus points to a larger animal, which takes us beyond even the wider definition of 'uterine'. But the quality of parchment derived from a heifer will have been finer than that from a mature animal. However, the very high quality achieved by the makers of Codex Sinaiticus is probably due to several causes. As well as giving credit to the skill of the manufacturers, we should consider also that they may have selected only the best out of many skins and that they used the highest quality ingredients throughout the processing. The rarity of skeletal marks suggests that usually a single animal provided two sheets, one being cut from each side. Occasionally a smaller animal yielded only one sheet, and then skeletal marks are sometimes visible (for example, on Q41-F4r).

The parchment used for Codex Sinaiticus is of exceptionally high quality. Most manuscripts contain a number of leaves with holes in them. These are either places where the animal had suffered trauma or the result of damage in the preparation process. In Codex Sinaiticus there are only a few, all of small size, and usually in a margin. (The parchment maker sometimes sewed them up when the skins were wet, and sometimes they were repaired by somebody at a later stage, by pasting a thin piece of parchment over the hole.) The difficulty of identifying veins indicates that the blood was expertly drained from the carcass after slaughter. The thinness and quality of the parchment has led to speculation that the manufacturers used some otherwise unknown method, or even that they worked out a lost technique of splitting calf skin into two sheets (which is believed to be possible only with sheep skin). What is certain is that the makers were exceptionally skilled, and that they worked with excellent materials. It is clear that no expense was spared. It would be too much to say that there was never another such manuscript in the fourth century. We can only say that there is no surviving manuscript to compare with it. Other manuscripts whose parchment shows high manufacturing standards include Codex Vaticanus and Codex Bezae (which was produced a little later, in around the year 400).

Codex Bezae contains the Gospels and Acts in Greek with a parallel Latin translation.

A good page for observing the process of turning animal into parchment is Q62-F2r, zones e (the top) and g (the bottom). Looking first with high magnification at the image made under standard light, one may see the dark pimples of hair follicles on the bottom of the lower margin. Also in the lower margin are axilla marks. The axilla is the stretchier and looser area of skin between the beast's fore and hind legs on each side. The indicators of this are a wavier parchment, and widening spacing between the follicles. Moving up to the top margin, above the first column, the slightly darker traces of veins are visible (but easily confused with creases). Finally, there is a round hole in the bottom right hand corner. This is a scar from the skin of the living animal (it was repaired with a sliver of

See Plate 4a

See Plate 4b

parchment). The next trace is of the preparation process. The hole has a mark from the scraping process right through the scar, more or less horizontally. The area may have been avoided during the scraping process, so that the material was thicker here. In the final stage of scraping, it may be that the parchment maker's blade caught on extruding tissue and then jagged in.

Follicles, axilla marks, veining and scar tissue are all connections between this smooth writing surface and its origins.

Under raking light and before the image is magnified, the greater waviness of the bottom edge may be seen. Under high magnification, the follicles in the bottom margin are much clearer than they are under standard light, and it is easier to observe the way in which they get further apart toward the edge. The veins are scarcely visible. The scar and the striation mark, on the other hand, have the appearance of a crevasse. The very fine parchment added by the manufacturer shows clearly as a rough square glued over the circle.[1]

The skin of Codex Sinaiticus is very thin indeed. The Conservation Assessment undertaken as part of the Project records the thickness of each leaf as measured with a caliper at seven places. If we take the example of the first leaf of Quire 35, we find that the thickness varies between 100 and 150 micrometres,[2] with an average of 116.2. By comparison, the pages of this book are 125 microns thick. There are a few manuscripts of a similar age which are nearly as fine, but the parchment of large books was soon to become markedly thicker. It is remarkable that one of the oldest parchment manuscripts should also be of such fine quality. Was the method used to produce it already in use for some other purpose, or was it especially developed for parchment production? It is precisely the fineness of the parchment that makes Codex Sinaiticus possible. Given the opulent layout, which will be discussed below, one needed thin material for the Codex to be of manageable size.

See Plate 4c

[1] Other good places for observing striation and/or follicle marks are Q40-F1v (zone e), Q41-F1v (g for follicles and e-c-d for striation), Q42-F2r (e) and Q45-F4r (g–f).

[2] A micrometre, commonly known as a micron, is one thousandth of a millimetre.

MARKING UP THE LAYOUT

The prepared parchment is not yet ready to receive writing. A very important task awaits the scribes: planning the page layout of the codex, and setting it out on the leaves with pricked holes and lines made with a dry point. The dry point would make an indentation through the sheets. The process was one in which scribes were very conservative. It began with the four sheets of a quire being laid flat in a pile. In Greek codices the first sheet was placed hair side up, the second flesh side up, the third hair side up, and the fourth flesh side up. They were then folded in half to make a booklet of eight leaves and sixteen pages. The outer pages of this booklet were flesh side, and each inner opening was alternately hair and flesh. The purpose of this was visual, since the hair side tends to be darker and to absorb ink better. The scribe then made the prickings, so that a single set of prickings for the horizontal lines served for both ends, since the horizontal lines were ruled with the pages opened out again. So the procedure was:

> take four sheets with alternately hair and flesh facing up
> fold them in half
> prick them
> unfold them
> make the vertical and horizontal lines

Was a template used for the pricking? This would be the obvious way to go about it. Initial evidence suggests that the prickings for the main outline may have been made with a template (in order to achieve overall uniformity) and those for the horizontal lines of the text blocks without one. Compare, for example, the two quires 76 and 77. The vertical prickings of the text (to be seen towards the end of the lines in column 4 of the recto) are markedly different if one sets them both against a notional straight line. It is also noticeable that the positioning of the prickings for the vertical lines varies a good deal in relation to the top and bottom margins (compare Quires 57 and 58 for example).

The lines were inscribed on the unfolded sheets because to do so when they were folded (which would have needed half the number of actions) would have required potentially damaging pressure on the top leaf, in order to make an impression all the way through.

There are two different layouts: one with four columns which was used generally, and one with two which was used for the poetical books: Psalms, Proverbs, Ecclesiastes, Song of Songs, Wisdom of Solomon, Sirach and Job (448 pages, more than a third of the whole). Each column is marked with a vertical line on either side, and with horizontal ones to guide the writing. Sometimes these are marked for every line of writing, sometimes for two and sometimes for four. For each vertical line a pricking hole was made at top and bottom, for each horizontal line a pricking hole at each end. These were hidden by being placed inside what would become the written area of the outside columns of the sheet. See for example Q76-F1r, where they are well inside the ends of the outside column. For the running titles, a hole was pricked in one of the innermost vertical lines at the point where it should go (see Q74-F1r, where in fact there are two).

All the data is now available for a thorough analysis of the whole process of sheet preparation in the manufacture of the Codex. But it will be some time before the study is completed.

THE INK

The ink used for writing the Codex was of two colours, brown and red. The brown ink in which most of the text is written is tannin-based, containing perhaps oak gall, perhaps bark. Sometimes the use of an acidic ink has led to serious damage to the parchment of ancient manuscripts. Here, however, the material has generally remained stable, except in some of the New Finds and Leipzig leaves which have been exposed to high moisture levels (water damage is more likely than humidity as regards the New Finds, given the desert setting of St Catherine's). The red ink was used for headings in the Psalms and for chapter numbers and other numbering systems.

This was already an old custom. There is a fragment of Psalms from among the Dead Sea Scrolls which has the first two lines of each psalm in red.

THE SCRIBES

The materials are ready. For whom? What do we know about the people who produced Codex Sinaiticus, and about their working conditions? In the first place, they were a team. We know this from differences in manufacture between different parts of the manuscript. This includes the handwriting itself, and the quality and distinctive characteristics of each part. How many scribes were there? Here opinion has been divided. Tischendorf found four, whom he named A, B, C and D. He attributed the prophetic books to B, the poetical books and Hermas to C, Tobit and Judith and some other leaves to D and most of the rest to A. Subsequent scholarship generally accepted this. But Milne and Skeat reduced the number to three, the leaves attributed to C being reassigned to D and A. In the course of the Project, it has been proposed that B is not one but two scribes, B1 and B2, the latter copying the Twelve Prophets and Hermas. If we include the leaves of the New Finds, we have the following table of scribes:

A   Leviticus, Numbers, Deuteronomy, Joshua, Judges,
    1 Chronicles, 2 Esdras, Esther, 1 Maccabees, 4 Maccabees
    8.7–end, Psalms 97.3–end, Proverbs, Ecclesiastes, Song of
    Songs, Wisdom, Sirach, Job, all the New Testament except
    for a few leaves written by D (see below), and Barnabas
B1 Isaiah, Jeremiah and Lamentations
B2 The Twelve Prophets and Hermas
D   Genesis, Tobit, Judith, 4 Maccabees 1.1–8.7, Psalms 1.1–97.3,
    Matthew 16.9–18.12, 24.36–26.6, Mark 14.54–Luke 1.56,
    1 Thessalonians 2.14–end, Hebrews 4.16–8.1, Revelation 1.1–5

In the number of pages written, their workload was

A   995 (including duplication of fourteen pages)
B   324 (B1 206 and B2 118)
D   167

This assumes that the scribe responsible for extant fragments in the Pentateuch copied that book in its entirety, that A copied Exodus, that B1 copied Ezekiel and Daniel and that B2 copied all of the Twelve Prophets.

But we have to set this evidence in a somewhat wider context, namely the supplementary apparatus – items such as running titles, names before and after books and numberings – and the in-house correction process which was carried out before the book was released. These show that B (one cannot distinguish between B1 and B2 in these) provided running titles in a number of books; that D corrected A's work but A never corrected D's; that B alone was responsible for the copying and correction of B's Old Testament text; and that A, B (one or both) and D had a hand in the Pauline letters. This indicates a continuous process of give and take, of piles of sheets being passed from one scribe to another to have some part of the business finished off.

Was D the senior scribe?

It is arguable that D was in some ways senior, perhaps supervising the other two. The evidence for this is that his work is of a higher quality than theirs, and that he quite often corrects it, sometimes even writing replacement leaves. Did D copy the first book as a model, so that the opening pages should be of the best quality? And did D also copy the first three and a half quires of the poetical books for A to imitate in the rest?

Some problems with B's delivery

B (taking this as a single scribe) is the least satisfactory, showing poorer spelling than the other two. Was B given less work because of these difficulties? Alternatively, Scribe B may have been a part-timer, or working on other productions, and was only brought in to this project occasionally. If Scribe B is divided into two, the possibility that this scribe or these scribes were brought in occasionally is stronger, since the entire copying process will have taken longer than their contribution. It suggests also that the two blocks of the Major and Minor Prophets may have been copied simultaneously.

We should envisage a team of three or more scribes. One evident reason for this is that they could copy different parts of the text at the same time. Another aspect of the whole task must therefore have been allocation of blocks and planning of workflow. As will become clear, this part of the enterprise did not always work very well.

But the time has come for some important explanations. Quite a lot of information has been given without any explanation: 'Codex Sinaiticus was copied in the middle of the fourth century.' Why do we say so? 'There were four scribes'. How can we tell? It is time to justify these claims.

PALAEOGRAPHY

If we get a handwritten letter in the post, we may recognise the handwriting. I would immediately know a letter from my brother or one from my sister. It is much harder to distinguish between two professional scribes writing in a particular style. But palaeography, a discipline first developed in France in the late seventeenth century, provides the tools for making informed judgements.

First of all, one can get some idea from the general shape of the letters. This has to be treated carefully. Since scribes were trained to write in particular ways, two scribes might have written letters in a very similar manner. Even when one considers not the shape, but the precise sequence in which the strokes of the letter are written, there is room for uncertainty. Moreover, one may expect some degree of unevenness across hundreds of pages even in the most expert of scribes, so that two pages from opposite ends of a manuscript may look disconcertingly as though they were by different scribes, even though an examination page by page shows no change in style. Even so, letter formation is the place to start when discerning different hands. Kappa (K) is one of the most revealing letters for distinguishing between our scribes.

Secondly, scribes have distinctive habits which are unconscious, and so harder than letter shapes to control. One is the way in which they compress text at the ends of lines, either by writing small, or combining letters, in order to be able to break words across lines according to the rules. D is distinctive in the use of the caret, a space filler like an angle bracket.

See Plate 6

51

Thirdly (and this departs from palaeography), one can observe idiosyncrasies in the way the scribes reproduce the text: the quality of their spelling, the typical errors that they make, the frequency with which they introduce new paragraphs.

The script

Palaeographers of Greek make a broad distinction between documentary hands and book hands. The former were used for most purposes, including writing letters, general administration, and so on. Book hands were used for making fine copies of literary texts. From an early date, de luxe copies were made of works such as the *Iliad* and *Odyssey*, and some examples of these papyrus rolls survive. The oldest Christian manuscripts do not pretend to this grandeur, and are written in a variety of hands, concentrating for the most part on speed and economy (with the aim of reducing both time and materials as far as possible). In the fourth century, however, there emerged the form of Greek writing called biblical majuscule, which was to dominate Christian books for several centuries. Majuscule indicates that what we would today call upper case letters are used (later the minuscule script developed, using the precursors of lower case letters). Not all the characters of biblical majuscule are the same as the modern equivalent.

> Theta, xi and omega are written in the same way as their modern lower case forms (θ, ξ, ω)
> Sigma is written in the lunate form (c)

The characteristics of biblical majuscule are that the characters are written within a notional square and with thick vertical strokes and very fine horizontals.

Dating manuscripts

Unfortunately, ancient scribes did not put the date when they began or finished a piece of work. The oldest surviving dated manuscript of the Greek Bible is a copy of the Gospels written in 835. In the

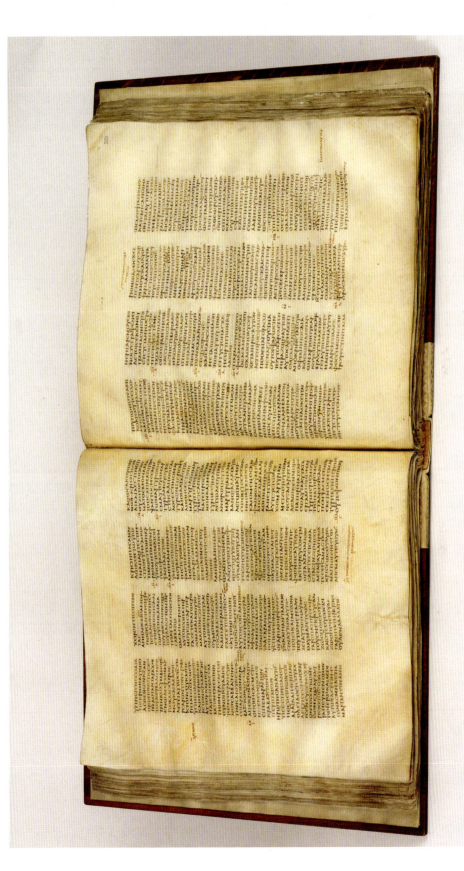

1 A full opening of Codex Sinaiticus, showing John 5.6–6.23 (Q80-F3v and F4r).

2 St Catherine's Monastery, Sinai, depicted on the back of the archbishop's throne.

3 A papyrus (British Library Pap. 2484) showing John 16.14–22. It dates from the third century.

4a Q62-F2r: hair follicles in the lower margin.

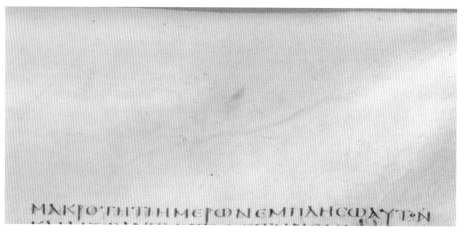

ΜΑΚΡΟΤΗΤΗΗΜΕΡωΝΕΜΠΛΗСωΑΥΤΟΝ

4b Q62-F2r: veining in the upper margin.

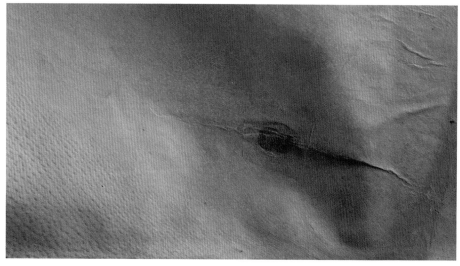

4c Q62-F2r: a hole repaired by the manufacturer, and a knife cut made in the preparation process (raking light image).

5a Q35-F4v-C4: The 'three crosses note' marking the end of the repeated section of fourteen pages.

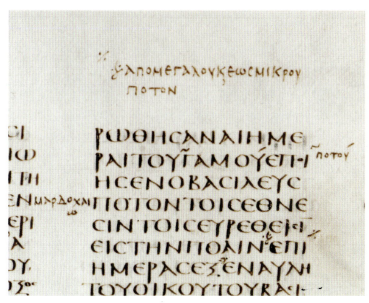

5b An addition in the top margin. The symbol three letters in from the end of line 6 shows where it belongs (Q36-F5v-C3).

6a Scribe A (Q76-F3v-C1).

6b Scribe B1 (Q46-F3v-C4).

6c Scribe B2 (Q57-F4r-C4).

6d Scribe D (Q37-5v-C2).

7 Q77-Frv: a general view (image does not include all of the top and bottom margins).

8 Q77-F1v: a close-up of the top of column 1.

absence of such evidence, palaeographers have worked out a process of comparison, moving from the more to the less certain. The kinds of evidence that help are the following:

first, and most obviously, the content of a manuscript has to post-date that content's composition. This content may be the text itself, or a particular edition or presentation of the text;

second, a roll may have had a documentary text with a date in it written on the back, so it must have been written before that date; or something may have been written in a margin or at the beginning or end of a codex that serves the same purpose;

thirdly, where there are several scribes involved in the production of a manuscript, or where there are distinctive corrections, the evidence from several hands may lead to a more precise dating;

fourthly, any artwork in the manuscript can be dated by an art historian;

fifthly, the copy may have physical characteristics which are significant: a paper manuscript is unlikely to pre-date the twelfth century; a parchment codex will not pre-date the fourth;

sixthly, there may be particular historical circumstances which provide a possible context for a particular kind of production

From whatever fixed points emerge, and out of a careful compari-son of every surviving document, a framework has slowly been developed. Each manuscript contributes a part to the sum of our knowledge.

Of the six kinds of evidence listed above, the first helps us to date Codex Sinaiticus. The scribes included in the Gospels a system of paragraph numbering devised by Eusebius of Caesarea. The precise date of the system is unknown, but the probable chronology of Eusebius' life indicates that it cannot have been earlier than about 320. Moreover, the incomplete and unconvincing way in which the system is presented in Codex Sinaiticus suggests that it had not yet become well known to scribes.

Dating a manuscript written as long ago as the fourth century cannot be done with the precision that we would wish. We have to allow for the general possibility that a scribe may have written in a particular manner throughout a career which might have lasted, for all we know, for fifty years, and we must acknowledge that changes in scripts may not have been adopted and abandoned at the same time in every place.

The standard work on biblical majuscule dates Codex Sinaiticus to '360 or a little later'. A date much earlier is ruled out by the 'refined elegance' of the script and the decorative elements. A date much later is ruled out by immediate changes in the script. According to the same writer, Codex Vaticanus was made in about 350. It is a theory which owes a lot to a schema according to which biblical majuscule evolved, achieved a perfect canonical form, and then fell into decline. This may be too rigid a concept. But the dating of Codex Sinaiticus to the middle of the century is generally agreed.

Separating manuscripts by a decade at such a remove may be over-confident. The best we can say is that the evidence such as it is leads us to believe that Codex Sinaiticus may have been written shortly after the middle of the fourth century.

Can we say whether Codex Sinaiticus is older than Codex Vaticanus? Scholars have often argued without any sound evidence that Codex Vaticanus is older, so why should one not suggest the opposite?

A scriptorium

The activity of a group of scribes suggests that the manuscript was made in a scriptorium, a book copying workshop. Here it is important to clear up a common confusion. Scriptoria were places dedicated to book production. But they were not places of mass production as we would understand it today. It is often imagined that books were written to dictation, one person reading out the text as a number of others wrote down the words, so that a number of copies could be made simultaneously. There is no evidence that this ever happened, and there are some practical difficulties to be considered. The idea that a number of people wrote while a single person read is founded on the theory that this practice would have been successful economically. The theory presupposes two things: first that the book trade was like today's, with copies stocked by booksellers, but in fact the evidence suggests that in late antiquity books were usually written to order. Second that if a number of scribes wrote at once it would save time, but again this is not so certain. Such a practice would have required every scribe to write at the speed of the slowest, so the quicker scribes will have wasted time by having to work below their optimum speed. It will also have involved the work of one extra person, the reader. We have therefore to abandon this fanciful concept, and try to work out how our team did go about their task.

Who were the scribes?

A, B and D are disappointingly anonymous names. Can we flesh them out any further? The degree of information about their class is generally slight. Readers are interested in the book, not the person who produces it, and it is likely that the less the scribe was noticed, the better the job.

According to one source, a scribe will have been born under Gemini, along with philologists, teachers, poets, lovers of the arts and businessmen. Whether our scribes were Christian we do not know, although there is no reason to suppose that if they were they would have been any more or less confident in their star signs. It is common to refer to a scribe as 'he', but 'she' is also possible. We know of several groups of female scribes. Origen had at his disposal a large team of writers in shorthand and copyists including girls trained in writing well. In the course of the fourth century, those taking up the monastic life found it a suitable one for copying texts. Rufinus' friend Melania the Elder copied for a fixed time every day, and wrote codices 'very well and fluently'. Her products included copies of both testaments. A variety of other female scribes, both slave and free, are mentioned in Roman inscriptions. Among the few relevant Greek inscriptions, one records a girl who won a calligraphy contest. But we do not know what proportion of scribes were women, and we have no way of knowing whether *our* scribes are male or female, young or old, enslaved or free, Christian or pagan. We have

Rufinus (c. 345–411) translated many Greek works into Latin, most notably writings by Origen. Melania was a wealthy Roman lady who adopted the monastic life in Palestine.

55

only the record of their activity, a record which tells us that they were expert at writing, but of mixed ability when it came to copying.

COLLECTING THE SOURCE MATERIALS

To understand the circumstances of production, we have to consider how the scribes used the sources from which they copied the new manuscript. Every manuscript is a copy of one or more other manuscripts. In most circumstances, the task involved a straight copying of one to another. For example, a complete copy of the Gospel of Luke will have been copied to make another complete copy of the Gospel of Luke. But the scribes of Codex Sinaiticus had a more complicated task. They had to assemble one codex out of a shelf-ful of books. For the New Testament, this may have consisted of anything between six and ten individual codices (more if the Catholic Epistles were not available in a single codex). We may suppose that at the very least they may have had one copy containing the Gospels, one of Acts and the Catholic Epistles, one of Paul's letters, one of Revelation, one of Barnabas and one of Hermas, six in total. Ten gives them a separate copy of each of the Gospels and separate copies of Acts and the Catholic Epistles.

See page 16.

For the Old Testament, they might have required twenty-four manuscripts. We do not know whether the scribes used any rolls for the Old Testament books. If they did, then they will have had an even more difficult task working out the size and layout of their codex.

The scribes may therefore have had to gather up to three dozen manuscripts. It is interesting to speculate whether or not they were able to find all the texts they wanted. About the year 400 someone wrote to Jerome asking for help in tracking down manuscripts of certain Old Testament books so that he could have copies made of those which he did not possess. Codex Sinaiticus contains 1 and 4 Maccabees, but not the second and third books. Is this because the scribes could not find copies of these books?

PLANNING THE CODEX

These thirty or so exemplars were presumably produced by as many different scribes, may have been written some on papyrus and some on parchment, were perhaps a mixture of rolls and codices, in different scripts, with differences in spelling, punctuation habits and quality and with different layouts. The scribes had to make a series of decisions which would bring all these things into a consistent whole:

> technical standards, including determining the size, quality and preparation of the parchment and the type and consistency of the inks
>
> page layout, including the number of columns on a page and the size of each column
>
> how to indicate new paragraphs, and what punctuation to use
>
> how to present running titles and the superscriptions and subscriptions (these are the short titles at the beginning and end of each book)
>
> what ornamentation to use, especially the forms of the coronae (the decorations at the ends of books)
>
> where to use red ink
>
> what script to use
>
> how to present the ancillary material (things like the Eusebian apparatus in the Gospels and chapter numbers)
>
> how to divide the labour (this required calculating the number of pages needed for each block of material)

For many individual features, the scribes may have been totally dependent upon the manuscript of a particular book that was available to them. For example, if it contained chapter numbers, they could be included; if it did not, they would be lacking in Codex Sinaiticus.

Sharing the work

Imagine you have agreed with a colleague that you will copy a block of text which has to finish at the end of a quire. The most important consideration is layout, and here we see how important visual judgement is to a scribe, who has to look at the exemplar, calculate how much text is in it, and then mentally revisualise this amount to fit a completely new layout. We can understand the problem by looking at a few places where they ran into difficulties.

Scribe B1 wrote Isaiah, which begins at Quire 43. This work had probably begun before the historical books had been finished. The evidence for this is found in the last part of the historical books, from Quires 37 to 42, which contain some interplay between A and D. It looks as though when Scribe A finished Esther, on Q37-F3r-C2, it was decided that D would take over Tobit and Judith, and A would jump ahead to 1 Maccabees. This required a calculation of the amount of space needed for these two books, so that they would know where A should begin again. Tobit begins on Q37-F3r-C3 and 1 Maccabees begins on Q39-F3r-C2. So they must have worked out that Tobit and Judith together would occupy thirty-one pages and three columns. But this turned out to be too generous. Scribe D realised this once he got into Quire 39: the second folio has only forty-six or forty-seven lines to a column instead of the usual forty-eight, and there are a greater number of fillers (carets) to pad out the text. Even so, the text was too short to fill the last column allocated (Q39-F3r-C1), which had to be left blank.

If the plan was for Scribe A to write 1 and 4 Maccabees so as to finish all the historical books, it had to be revised. Perhaps D copied faster than A, because we now find him starting 4 Maccabees – on a new quire. This new quire was achieved by adjusting the length of the last gathering of 1 Maccabees, making it out of two sheets instead of the usual four.

At the same time, 4 Maccabees was also fitted into a single quire, and this is the evidence that Scribe B1 had already written or started to write the prophetic books, beginning on a new quire. Being committed to keeping 4 Maccabees on a single quire, D realised on Q42-F3 that he needed to compress the text, and started writing 50 instead of 48 lines in a column, increasing this to 53 lines in the last two columns of Q42-F4r. Then, after D had written seven pages, A took over on Q42-F4v, maintaining the 50-line rate for three pages, and dropping down to 48 for the last three, achieving a neat end near the bottom of the last column of the quire.

Why did A take over the end of 4 Maccabees? Perhaps because he had finished 1 Maccabees, and D needed to move on: one may speculate he needed to start writing the specimen section of the poetical books.

A similar problem arose in the books Revelation–Barnabas–Hermas. Here too there is a change of scribe: A ended one quire with Barnabas, and B started the next with Hermas. So we may suppose that A had again the task of finishing Barnabas within a quire. But something strange happened. Barnabas is written in two quires, one of three sheets (twelve pages) and one of a single sheet (four pages). The first quire (91) is made up wrongly, consisting of the first, third and fourth sheets of a regular four-sheet quire (we know this because the openings Q91-F1v/2r and Q91-F5v/6r are not matching hair and matching flesh as they should be, but hair/flesh and flesh/hair respectively). Perhaps Scribe A originally finished Revelation on Q90-F2r and began Barnabas on the verso (leaving three columns blank). He then realised that Barnabas would not fit onto the rest of the quire, took out the original second sheet and rewrote the end of Revelation on the first column of the third sheet, beginning Barnabas on the second column. But Barnabas still needed an extra sheet which had to be supplied as an extra single-sheet quire.

Again, we find a scribe, this time B(2), writing a block of text before the previous one was finished. What explanations are there for this? One is that time is money. If one had a team working on manuscript production, one needed to keep them fully occupied. Alternatively, they may have been up against a deadline.

The scribe could have simply replaced the original second sheet with the one that was used for Quire 92.

Traces of older scribes

Sometimes, we find places where a scribe has copied a feature of the source manuscript which no longer makes sense in its new setting. This is a possible explanation of the occasional appearance of four dots, used either as a filler or as a punctuation marker:

> five times in Jeremiah (Scribe B1) (Q47-F1r-C4-L5, 47-4r-4-20, 8-8r-1-5, 48-8v-4-26 (one in the left and one in the right margin))
> twice in the Minor Prophets (Scribe B2) (Q57-F5r-C1-L15, 57-6r-2-21)
> twice in Acts (Scribe A) (Q87-F5r-C3-L37, 87-5v-1-40)

Even more striking is the appearance of three dots and a line, found only at Q82-F4r-C2-L38. By contrast, the use of three dots is quite common. It comes fifteen times in Romans and once in Acts. Are these occasional relics of practices found in exemplars, or even left over in them from previous stages, or are they occasional conscious scribal decisions? Why should there be fifteen triple dots in Romans, but nowhere else in the Pauline collection? Since, as we have seen, these may reasonably be expected to have all been copied from one codex, why are they not uniformly spread? There are several possible explanations. The fact that Romans is the first letter in the collection may be significant. There is at present no way of determining whether the feature has any significance at all. A lot more sifting of the evidence, in search of matching patterns, would have to be done before any conclusions could be reached. But it is worth pointing out how much easier such study is with an electronic version. I am able to search the XML of the entire transcription and find all occurrences of such patterns within a few seconds. The possibility of piecing together the complex structural history of a manuscript like Codex Sinaiticus is now within our grasp.

FINISHING THE JOB

Binding

The last stage in a book's production is to bind it. There are very few surviving examples of fourth-century bookbindings. Those from the collection of Coptic books found at Nag Hammadi have leather bindings. Some evidence remains of the way in which Codex Sinaiticus was originally stitched together. Cockerell, rebinding the manuscript after 1934, found a few surviving 'single threads of loosely twisted hemp', but no evidence of the way in which the leaves were sewn. The manuscript was rebound at least once, and possibly twice, between then and the twentieth century.

Navigation

The first codex-makers devised various options for finding one's way around a manuscript, including a table of contents, though unfortunately whatever Codex Sinaiticus may ever have had in that department is now lost. It was also possible to mark the beginning of each book with a tab, a tie-on label, one might say, attached to the first page of the book, on which its name would be written. The labels are no longer present, but Codex Sinaiticus contains the pin-hole and sometimes even the thread which went through it. They were at different positions on the page, so that the tabs would not obscure each other. At some later date, they were replaced with ones which were glued to the page, of which some traces remain.

Reconstruction of the lost initial section reveals that Genesis 1.1 began on Q2-F1r, so the first quire must have contained prefatory material of some kind.

THE BUDGET

One thing which the scribes (or someone) should have done before they started was to work out the budget. In 301, the Emperor Diocletian issued an edict stating what everything should cost. The parts of the edict which have survived include regulations for leather and writing:

> to a parchment-maker for a foot-square quire of parchment or yellow parchment, 40 denarii
> to a scribe for best writing, 100 lines, 25 denarii
> for second quality writing, 100 lines, 20 denarii
> to a notary for writing a petition or legal document, 100 lines, 10 denarii

By translating from the denarii of the edict into a more durable value such as gold or wheat, it may be possible to work out the cost of making Codex Sinaiticus.

There is a story from the fourth or fifth century of a complete parchment Bible which was worth eighteen solidi and John Moschus (c. 550–619) writes of a New Testament worth three solidi. Since the Septuagint is six times as long as the New Testament, these figures are a precise match, although we do not know whether the manuscripts were of the same quality.

A solidus would have bought you 266 or 267 sheets of best-quality foot-square parchment, but since Codex Sinaiticus is larger than that, we must suppose that its 743 sheets would have cost more than 2.8 solidi. It has been calculated that a Bible written on foot-square parchment would have comprised 1,533,600 square cm of writing material, costing 3.2 solidi. Calculating the unit value per square cm for the 2,428,124 square cm of the surface area of Codex Sinaiticus gives a cost for its parchment of 5.1 solidi.

Turning to the copying, between 136 and 137,000 lines of the length mentioned in the edict (for parchment of that dimension) would have been needed to copy a Bible. Codex Sinaiticus had 224 pages with two columns, the remaining 1,262 having four. If we assume that, given their unusual brevity, every page was counted as having two, we would have 142,656 lines. This translates into a cost of 13.6 solidi. We arrive then at these very tentative figures:

Cost of parchment	5.1 solidi
Labour	13.6 solidi
Binding	1 solidus
Total	19.7 solidi

The total cost when compared with the value of wheat translates into approximately four and three quarter imperial tons and metric tons and just over 5 US tons. The cost in loaves per page before binding is between six and seven. It has been suggested that the

A solidus was a gold coin introduced in the fourth century which weighed about 4.5 grams of gold.

We do not know whether the larger unit size actually cost more per square cm, but at least this gives us an upper limit according to this computation.

This is enough wheat to produce 10,500 loaves of a pound weight.

annual income of priests and deacons at the time was between 20 and 25 solidi a year.

These figures are of course tentative. But they provide further evidence that Codex Sinaiticus was beyond the ordinary.

SOURCES AND FURTHER READING

The description of the parchment on Q62-F2r was provided by Gavin Moorhead of the British Library Conservation Department, one of the team who examined each page of the manuscript in intense detail. I also made extensive use of the report by Christopher Clarkson on the New Finds, which he kindly made available to me, and of the report by John Mumford on the conservation of the London leaves in 'The Codex Sinaiticus Project: 2. Conservation Work', in G. Fellows-Jensen and P. Springborg (eds), *Care and Conservation of Manuscripts 10: Proceedings of the Tenth International Seminar held at the University of Copenhagen 19th–20th October 2006*, Copenhagen: Museum Tusculanum Press, 2008, pp. 153–71.

For the fourth scribe, I made use of Amy Myshrall's privately circulated paper 'The Presence of a Fourth Scribe in Codex Sinaiticus' (October 2006).

The authority on biblical majuscule is G. Cavallo, *Ricerche sulla maiuscola biblica* (Studi e testi di papirologia 2), 2 vols, Florence: Le Monnier, 1967, with 115 plates. The quotation is my translation from page 60.

The correspondence with Jerome is taken from his Letter 5.

The papyrus listing the star signs of different professions is quoted in Peter Parsons' magnificent account of Oxyrhynchus as it is known from its papyri: *City of the Sharp-Nosed Fish. Greek Lives in Roman Egypt*, London: Weidenfeld and Nicolson, 2007, p. 187.

For female scribes, see K. Haines-Eitzen, *Guardians of Letters. Literacy, Power and the Transmitters of Early Christian Literature*, New York: Oxford University Press, 2000, Chapter 2.

Cockerell's comments on the original binding may be found on page 82 of Milne and Skeat's *Scribes and Correctors*.

The details from Diocletian's prices edict are taken from S. Lauffer (ed.), *Diokletians Preisedikt* (Texte und Kommentare 5), Berlin: De Gruyter, 1971.

The calculations on which I have drawn are found in R. S. Bagnall, *Early Christian Books in Egypt*, Princeton and Oxford, 2009, 50–62. I am also grateful to Professor Bagnall for a private communication on the subject.

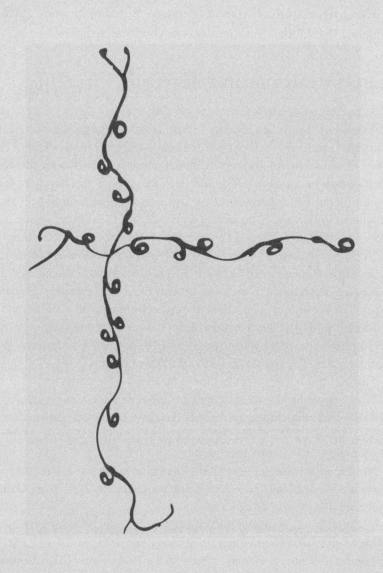

CHAPTER FIVE

The Scribes and What They Did

WE NOW have four scribes; D, who was probably in charge; A, who did most of the work; and B1 and B2, who did their work the least well. To understand what we have in front of us, we need to try to trace their activity as carefully as possible. We need to think in blocks of text, relating that to the physical layout and understanding their decisions.

By 'block of text' I mean the longer textual units, such as a book or group of books.

A PROBLEM IN 2 ESDRAS

Because so little survives of the first part of the manuscript, there is very little to be said. There is nothing of Ruth or 1–4 Kingdoms (what we call the books of Samuel and Kings) and 2 Chronicles, and very little of the first seven books. The text proper begins in the middle of 1 Chronicles, and here immediately we notice an anomaly. The careful reader of the list of contents in Chapter 1 will have noticed that 1 Chronicles 17.14–17, 21–25; 18.1–4, 7–10, 12 appears twice. The explanation lies on Q35-F4v. As it now stands, there are three crosses placed at the bottom of the fourth column, followed by a note. The note is intended to cross-reference Line 26, where there are several deleted marks at the left of the line which may have been crosses. The note reads:

See Plate 5a

The sign of the three crosses marks the end of the seven redundant folios and is not part of Esdras.

65

The text changes from 1 Chronicles to 2 Esdras in the middle of Line 26, so that the first two words are from 1 Chronicles 19.17 and the last is from 2 Esdras 9.9. In the following English rendering of the lines in question, it is not difficult to identify where the switch occurs:

And it was told David; and he gathered all Israel, and passed over Jordan, and came upon them, and set the battle in array against them. So when David had put the battle in array against the Syrians, they fought with him the Lord our God and he hath extended mercy unto us in the sight of the kings of Persia, to give us a reviving, to set up the house of our God, and to repair the desolations thereof, and to give us a wall in Judah and in Jerusalem. (AV)

The note tells us that the seven folios (i.e. fourteen pages, of which five are extant) are a repetition of text that had already been copied. The scribe did not notice this confusion. The in-house corrector (who certainly read this page, making three corrections before the leap and two after) did not notice it. It is even possible that this page was checked by both A and D. No reader marked it until a later corrector finally spotted the mistake (see pages 80ff). How did they miss this piece of nonsense? And how did the scribe copy fourteen pages twice without noticing? The running titles to the repeated block of 1 Chronicles on Q35-F1r and F3r show that the scribe (A) *thought* he was copying 2 Esdras, and since they were probably added later, he had two chances (three, since he probably checked through these pages) to notice the problem.

We now have a better insight into what happened, because parts of the first copy of the text (also by Scribe A) is among the New Finds. Calculation of the missing pages shows that what happened was that the two books of Chronicles were copied, as was 1 Esdras. Then the scribe copied 2 Esdras until, when he got to 9.9, he copied a block of text from 1 Chronicles 6.57 (approximately) to 19.17.

It is often said that the most likely explanation is that the exemplar from which A was copying contained a block of text which had come from elsewhere. Perhaps it was a quire from another part of the manuscript, or from another manuscript, which had got bound in the wrong place. The fact that it is seven folios in Codex Sinaiticus might make it likely that it comprised a whole quire in a manuscript with a smaller size. But it is also possible that the exemplars were wholly or partly unbound, so that some of the 1 Chronicles copy found its way into the 2 Esdras copy. If this is so, then the scribe twice copied not just the same text, but the same copy of that text.

The difficulty for scribes and readers of dealing with this kind of problem is shown by the note, which places the three crosses at the bottom of the column, thereby implying that the text from Line 26 to the end is also not part of 2 Esdras (which of course it is).

One remaining question is how the scribe came to copy the block twice. In his defence, it must be said that he had seen this text some time ago, to be precise back on Quire 29, and here he is at the end of Quire 34 over sixty pages later. It would be unfair to claim that he must have copied without any attention to the actual content of the text in front of him. Clearly, he paid it great attention, even reproducing the impossible break in sense. And clearly he and D both corrected the manuscript against this same exemplar, and were satisfied that they had reproduced it precisely. This example there-fore tells us a great deal about the way in which the scribes worked, in particular about the way in which they set out to reproduce the copied text as carefully as possible, without necessarily ensuring that the text they were using was accurate.

HOW CONSISTENT WAS SCRIBE A?

We can learn even more when we compare the first and second copyings by the same scribe. This is a rather rare opportunity to test a scribe's consistency against himself. Such an assessment would be particularly useful if it was indeed the same exemplar which he used on both occasions, rather than two different copies of the same text. The verses 1 Chronicles 17.14–17 only survive in their first version in a damaged form, with the right hand part of each line missing. But we can immediately see that the line division is different in the two versions. There are differences in punctuation as well, with a new paragraph beginning at the start of verse 15 in the second copying but not the first. Further down, we find that a preposition differs in verse 16. The first version reads ΑΠΕΝΑΝΤΙ and the second ΑΠΕΝΑΝΤΙΟΝ (no knowledge of Greek is needed to spot the extra two letters the second time). Both forms are acceptable. At verse 21 we have a spelling variation: *lutrosasthai* the first time, *lutrosasthe* the second. These vowels were pronounced in the same way, *ai* sounding like a short e (*lutrosasthai* is correct). The very next word is intriguing. In the first version, the scribe correctly wrote *heautō*; the second time, he wrote *heauton ō*, which was later corrected to *heauton*. This looks like an uncertainty as to the right case ending for this reflexive pronoun. If there was some sort of confusion in the same exemplar, the scribe made a better job the first time.

One could carry on, but enough has been written to show that while the end products are very similar each time, there is a certain amount of what one might call 'noise', small changes to the presentation and wording but not to the sense.

Even if a recording is old and scratched, one may still recognise the tune.

We have now a good sense of the details of the copying process, the business of trying to get the text from one book into another without changing it too much in the process. But this transfer involved a new setting for the text, namely the new page layout. How the scribes achieved this has already been described. But it is worth spending a little time contemplating the results, looking at a page and seeing what there is on it.

LOOKING AT A PAGE

See Plate 7

I have chosen Q77-F1v, containing Mark 11.10–33. Because it is a hair side, the ink is very well set in the page; being in the New Testament, it is less heavily used than much of the Old Testament. And it does not contain any major corrections. In fact, it is about as close as we can get to a page as it left the scriptorium.

The evident items have already been covered: there are four columns, each with forty-eight lines. The top margin is smaller than the bottom margin, and the outer is larger than the inner. You may observe exactly the same in almost any book of any age. If the top and bottom margin were the same size, the text block would look as though it were put too low on the page. As it is, it looks just right. The smaller inner margin unites the two pages of the opening, which if the side margins were equal would look as though they were floating away from each other.

These dimensions may be regarded as the codicological equivalent of the balanced proportions which had been known in architecture for centuries.

The page has been computed to contain 2,541 characters, the columns containing 632, 609, 641 and 659 letters respectively. The average number of letters per line is therefore thirteen, but there is a variation of a letter a line between Columns 2 and 4.

Use of red ink

The ink of the main text block is in the darkish colour found throughout the manuscript, except for some red in the margins. These are numbers, in fact two sets of numbers, one above the other. The first consists of numbers dividing the Gospel into paragraphs (letters were often used to represent numbers; the first number against the first column, ρκ, means 120). The number below (in this case ς, i.e. 6) refers the reader to a table which cross-references the parallel paragraphs in whatever other Gospel or Gospels may contain the same material (these tables are missing in Codex Sinaiticus: they must have comprised the absent Quire 73 between Job and Matthew). The horizontal stroke above alerts the reader to the fact that these are numbers (see Column 1, Line 11, where the number 'twelve' is written as a numeral with a stroke over it, and a point either side for good measure: ·ιβ·).

See Plate 8

We cannot know whether Quire 73 was ever written, or whether it was removed later.

This 'Eusebian Apparatus' was added by Scribe D, perhaps as part of the final revision process.

Variety of display

If we look in detail at the first few lines of the first column, we will see the variety that the scribe brings to the display. There is the use of small characters at the end of a line to keep a fairly straight right margin and divide the word at an appropriate place: this includes writing the O in Lines 3 and 5 under the crossbar of the T, writing the E in Line 6 over the slope of the Λ, and in Line 1 simply writing the last two letters small. There is also the use of a superline over a final vowel to indicate a nu: see Line 2, where $\overline{A}$ stands for AN. In Line 12 there is a small o with a superline. There are other little tricks if we look across to Column 3: in Lines 4 and 10 the word και (= 'and') is abbreviated to the first letter with a stroke of the bottom right side of it: Ҟ. In Line 13, the letter sigma (c) where it comes three letters from the end is written very small.

Punctuation

Turning to punctuation, there is (by modern standards) a dearth. There is the indication of a new paragraph with a line hanging by about a letter's width in the left margin: see Line 4, with its initial K. There is sometimes a small space, as in the middle of Line 9, or after the first three letters of Column 4, Line 1. There is sometimes a point at the level of the tops of the letters, but many of these were added later, and there is not one on this page that looks original. There is sometimes a double point like a colon, as at the very bottom of Column 2, but the same caveat applies, and this example may not be original. Finally, there is the use of the diaeresis, the placing of two dots over iota (I) and upsilon (Y) when they are at the beginning of a word. The first example on this page comes over the Y which is the ninth letter of Line 3, then there are two over I at the end of the following line, and one over the final I of the fourth line.

But far and away the strangest thing to a modern reader is the fact that the words are written without any spaces, so that there is a continuous flow of letters. It seems to us obvious that words are separate units to be displayed in a way that makes this clear. But not so to the ancients. And perhaps they were right. Speak the text out loud as you read it, and your ear makes perfect sense of the text. This is exactly what was done in antiquity. While there is some debate about possible exceptions, the majority of the evidence clearly supports the view that people always spoke aloud as they read texts to themselves. The passage recounting the questioning of Christians which was quoted in Chapter Two reveals that a number of the church's books were at home with the lectors. An explanation for this is that they took the books home to prepare for reading. And perhaps like us they felt that the scribe had been a little mean with the punctuation, and added some as reminders to themselves of how they were going to deliver the text. In Codex Sinaiticus (as in other manuscripts) one may see punctuation in the form of dots squeezed where there is no obvious space and in a slightly different ink. This may be seen in Column 1 in

Line 2,	after $\overline{\text{ΔAΔ}}$
19	after AYTH
23	at the end of the line
48	after AYTOIC

There are still not very many, but one can imagine a reader adding punctuation in these places, two of which mark material introducing words of Jesus. Such marks are impossible to date, and they may as well have been added by private readers making sense of the text as in preparation for public recitation.

The sacred words

Another element to observe, one that is a distinctive feature of Christian biblical manuscripts, is the use of abbreviations for certain common names and nouns, many of them with a special connotation. They are abbreviated, often by contraction, with a line over the top. Examples on this page include:

Column	Line	written	means	English
1	2	$\overline{\text{ΔAΔ}}$	ΔAYEIΔ	David
2	31	$\overline{\text{IC}}$	IHCOYC	Jesus
	32	$\overline{\text{ΘY}}$	ΘEOY	of God

3	42	$\overline{\text{AN}\Omega\text{N}}$	ΑΝΘΡΩΠΩΝ	of men
	47	$\overline{\text{IY}}$	IHCOY	of Jesus

Other words usually abbreviated like this include Christ, Lord, Son, Father, Spirit, Israel, cross (and crucify), heaven. The complete set is known as the *nomina sacra*, the sacred words. There is no certain explanation for this custom, which is found even in the oldest surviving Christian manuscripts, but the result is that a number of very common special words are given special treatment in Christian books. Visually they stand out. Words in this category are not always sacral in connotation. For example, 'Lord' can still be abbreviated when the reference is to someone in authority and while 'man' in the phrase 'son of man' refers to Jesus in a very specific way, other references to 'man' and 'men', as here, have no special meaning. But the range of words in their narrow sense does suggest that there is something in their meaning which led early Christians to treat them in a unique way.

Scribal corrections

The process by which the scribes checked their own work – and D checked that of the others as well – has already been mentioned. There are only two examples on this page. In Column 1, Line 14, the scribe (A) realised when revising the text that he had omitted a word, and therefore needed to insert it. So ΕΠΙΝΑCΕΝ ('he hungered') is written in small letters above the place where it should be. Then in Column 4, Line 33, the scribe first wrote the nonsensical ΟΛΛΟΥC instead of ΑΛΛΟΥC. Again he corrected it later. (The corrector known as 'ca' later changed the way the correction was made.)

The line reads ΚΑΙΠΟΛΛΟΥCΟΛΛΟΥC. This is a good example of the way that similar series of letters could lead a scribe to repeat the first one.

This page does not contain everything that one can find in the Codex, and to complete the inventory we need to visit some other parts of it.

RUNNING TITLES

Step back a page to the previous opening, and the top margin contains a running title, divided across the two pages: KATA ('According to') on the left and MAPKON ('Mark') on the right. Coming on alternate openings, these running titles were written by Scribe A, probably after completing the text.

ORDERING THE PAGES

Over the years, the manuscript has acquired several series of numberings to keep the sheets in order. The oldest is a set of 'quire signatures' written in the top left hand corner of the first page of each quire. There is a clear example on the first complete quire, Q35-F1r, with a wavy line over it.

There is a second series of quire signatures, written in bold and dark ink, at the top right corner of the first page of each quire, and one can be seen on Q77-F1r. The number is oς, 76. These are accompanied by a binding mark, a vertical wiggly line in the middle of the right hand edge of the central opening of each quire. There is an example on Q36-F5r.

The two sets of signatures are identical in the Old Testament, but diverge by one in the New. The reason is the quire missing between the end of Job and the beginning of Matthew. The older set provides the evidence for that, moving from 72 to 74, but the second set has no break in it. This will be discussed below.

It is worth pausing for a moment longer with these quire signatures, because they provide more clues to the history of the manuscript.

It has been observed that the older set are not by any of the scribes. To be precise, they are not written in the formal hand of any of them. But they are written in quite an informal way, perhaps so as to be inconspicuous, certainly close enough to the top edge of the leaf to have been often lost in subsequent trimmings of the manuscript (once the manuscript had been bound they became redundant). The positioning, in line with the left bounding line, indicates that they belong to the original composition process (and it would be very hard to imagine so complicated a codex not conforming to the standard practice of including quire signatures). Either they were written quickly and informally by one of the known scribes, or there was someone else present in the scriptorium, who put the quires in the right order.

The second sequence, by contrast, is not at all discreet. These are quire signatures to be seen and admired. Boldly written in an unusual place (on the right top corner), they are ornamented with a variety of strokes. They are placed well in from the edge, so that they are at no risk from trimming. They may safely be dated to the eighth century. At that time then, it looks as though someone made a statement that this codex was in good hands, which might be interpreted as meaning both that it deserved honourable treatment, and that the owner (corporate or private) knew how to look after such a treasure.

Next to the second set of quire signatures is a much more modern feature, namely a set of folio numbers written in pencil, and running from 1 to 347. They are written on the top right corner of every recto that is in the British Library.

The Leipzig leaves are distinguished by a stamp on the bottom of each recto, and by the handwritten note in Tischendorf's hand at the top right corner of Q35-F1r:

Codex Friderico-Augustanus. 1845.

BEGINNINGS AND ENDS OF BOOKS

Each book has something at the beginning (the superscription) and end (the colophon, consisting of two items: the subscription stating the book's name, such as 'The Gospel according to Mark', and a decorative design known as the coronis). The variety of ways in which this is done tells us a surprising amount about the process by which the Codex was put together. In Mark, they were added by Scribe D. Each scribe had a distinctive way of writing the coronis, and this evidence combines with the script to give what has been called a 'completely decisive criterion' in deciding which scribe was responsible for a particular section.

See the black and white illustrations.

74

IN THE FOOTSTEPS OF THE SCRIBES

The observation of the way in which the books are named leads to the study of the way in which the scribes planned and executed their project. The importance of thinking in blocks of text, stated at the beginning of this chapter, comes to the fore here.

The pattern of scribal activity in writing the main text throughout the Codex has already been described. It consists of two blocks by B (1 and 2), and long stretches in which A wrote the main text blocks, with occasional bursts of activity by D.

The Codex is so designed that each major book or block begins on a new quire. This was achieved in several different ways. Once or twice it worked out just about right. Occasionally there had to be a little compression or expansion of the text density. Once or twice, and most drastically, the number of leaves in a gathering was reduced. For example, the last two sheets of Gathering 58 were cut out close to the gutter, so that Malachi ends on Q58-F6v and the Psalms begin on Q59-F1r. Working like this meant that in theory they could copy the books in any order and then bind them in the order that was eventually chosen.

The largest section was the entire set of historical books, which probably ran through complete quires all the way down to the adjustment in Quire 41 described above (by chance, the beginnings of 1 Kingdoms and Quire 20 coincided).

The major blocks that result are:

Quires 28 (?) to 42	1 Chronicles (?) to 4 Maccabees
Quires 43 to 58	Isaiah to Malachi (Joel begins a new quire after the missing Quires 50–56, but this is likely to be coincidence)
Quires 59 to 72	Psalms to Job
Quires 74 to 79	Matthew to Luke
Quires 80 to 81	John
Quires 82 to 91	Romans to Barnabas
Quires 92 to 96	Hermas

After the Gospels, the Codex has the rest of the New Testament in the order Paul's letters – Acts – the Catholic Epistles – Revelation.

These divide up quite obviously so far as the Old Testament is concerned, into:

historical books
prophetic books
poetical books

Matthew, Mark and Luke all cross over quires. But Q79-F8 is cut out, so that John begins on a new quire and the last two leaves of its last quire are cut out as well, so John is free-standing, and so too are the four Gospels. Here is a place where codicology (the study of the way a manuscript is put together and its text set out) can shed light on the history of texts and in this instance of religious thought. John, Origen's 'spiritual Gospel', stands alone in its own two quires. It is very tempting to see this as a way of according it special status within the entire collection.

The next block is one which is surprising in a different way. It consists of the fourteen letters of Paul, Acts, the Catholic Epistles, Revelation and Barnabas. One might expect breaks between Paul and Acts and between the Catholic Epistles and Revelation, and perhaps between Revelation and Barnabas. As it is, it looks as though the team regarded everything after the Gospels as an undifferentiated collection of letters, Acts and the Apocalypse (after all, it is still a far smaller block than any of those making up the Old Testament). Hermas starts on a new quire. This division was simply pragmatic, intended to allow Scribe B2 to copy it at the same time as A and D finished the preceding books.

SOURCES AND FURTHER READING

The statistics of letter numbers in Q77-F1v are taken from C. Tindall, *Contributions to the Statistical Study of the Codex Sinaiticus*, Edinburgh and London: Oliver and Boyd, 1961. I have not checked them.

The 'completely decisive criterion' was developed by Milne and Skeat (see page 27 of *Scribes and Correctors*). The places where the scribes seem to have struggled with dividing the work are discussed by Dirk Jongkind in *Scribal Habits*, pp. 41–47.

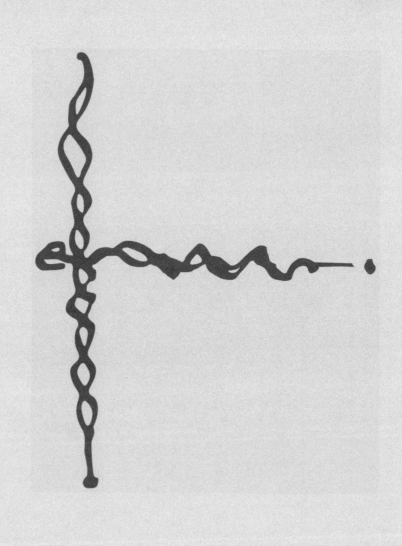

CHAPTER SIX

The Correctors and What They Did

THE differences between original and later entries in a manuscript are nothing like as obvious as they are in a printed book. In Codex Sinaiticus, we have a scribal text with scribal corrections, overlaid by later corrections. At each place (unless something has been very carefully erased), we can see what the text was initially, and to what it was changed. At each point of correction, the reader cannot but be aware of the existence of two or more wordings. The more corrections, the stronger this awareness.

It should be repeated that Codex Sinaiticus is unique among ancient manuscripts in the number of its corrections: a search in the Project's electronic transcription for the tag indicating a change to what was first written gives a list of 27,305 places where the text has been altered. This precise figure is an approximation, for several reasons. In the first place because, for technical reasons, a single correction spanning several verses has to be shown as a separate correction for each; in the second because different kinds of multiple corrections need separating into individual units in different ways; and in the third because it does not include places where a piece of text has been corrected more than once (of which there are over 3,000).

The detailed study of the correctors and their corrections is worthwhile, because of the insight it offers into the ways in which readers studied and used a biblical manuscript in antiquity; because learning the ability to differentiate between them provides an excellent palaeographical training; and because the study of the ways in which they altered the text can be used to document some of the details of how the text of the Old and New Testaments changed as time went by.

WHO WERE THE CORRECTORS?

As with the scribes, we have no personal information about the correctors, and must give them prosaic names. Because of weaknesses in the original identification of the correctors by Tischendorf, and because of inconsistencies in the selection of identifiers, the system is rather confusing (changing it would make matters worse). It becomes clearer once one knows what Tischendorf did. He divided all the correctors into five groups, A, B, C, D and E, and then distinguished between members of the groups. A and B denote the original three (or four) scribes. So the sequence of correctors begins with C.

An asterisk usually denotes the original scribe's original text. The usage cc* is an aberration.

Within it, they are called ca, cb, cc, cc* and cpamph. The group cb is represented by three identifiable hands, cb1, cb2 and cb3 (where one cannot distinguish between them, they are called cb). The most interesting is the one called cpamph.

Correctors may be dated in the same way as scribes. But there are two additional problems. The first is that correctors often write in cramped places, perhaps above the line, or between two letters of the original hand, and this can lead to distortion of their usual hand. The second is that it is very difficult to date corrections consisting only of a few letters at a time. To date the correctors of the Codex, one has to look for longer additions written in the margins. From these one may obtain dates down to the seventh century. The sequence of the correctors may be determined from the places where one of them changes a correction made by another.

THE PAMPHILIAN CORRECTOR

This name describes the supposed origin of the corrections, not the corrector. The corrector's work is found in two books only, 2 Esdras and Esther. There are 160 places of correction in the former, and 205 in the latter. They are often extensive, containing detailed corrections and insertions of missing text. A sample will be given shortly. The corrector supplied notes at the ends of the two books, explaining what had been done. The colophon to 2 Esdras reads as follows (Q34-F1r):

Collated against an extremely old copy corrected in the hand of the holy martyr Pamphilus, which copy at the end has a signature in his own hand, reading thus:
    Copied from and corrected against the Hexapla of Origen
    Antoninus collated
    I, Pamphilus, corrected

The colophon to Esther (Q37-F3r) is longer:

Collated against an extremely old copy corrected in the hand of the holy martyr Pamphilus. At the end of this very old book (which begins with the First Book of Kingdoms and ends at Esther) is the signature, in its distinctive form, of Pamphilus himself, reading thus:
    Copied from and corrected against the Hexapla of Origen as corrected by himself. Antoninus the confessor collated; I, Pamphilus, corrected the volume in prison, with the great favour and enlargement of God. And if it is not too much to say, to find a copy to match this one would not be easy.
The same very ancient book disagrees with this volume in the proper names

Origen and his Hexapla have already been described. Pamphilus was a pupil at Caesarea, in the tradition of Origen (his teacher Pierius was nicknamed 'Origen the Younger'), and became head of the school. Eusebius was his protégé (and seems to have become his spiritual son, renaming himself Eusebius of Pamphilus). Pamphilus was martyred in 309, during the Diocletianic persecution. The events were chronicled by Eusebius, in his *Church History* and in his *Martyrs of Palestine*. He also wrote a biography, which unfortunately has not survived. It appears that, along with a dozen of his

The last sentence was corrected by someone to read 'in some of the proper names'.

81

colleagues, Pamphilus was tortured and then imprisoned for two years (probably 307–09), at the end of which he again underwent torture and was put to death. An Antoninus who was beheaded is mentioned in *The Martyrs of Palestine*, but there is no way of knowing whether he is the person mentioned in the colophon.

According to Eusebius, Pamphilus was

a man who through his entire life was celebrated for every virtue, for renouncing and despising the world, for sharing his possessions with the needy, for contempt of earthly hopes, and for philosophic deportment and exercise. He excelled all his contemporaries in the sincerest devotion to the Divine Scriptures and indefatigable industry in whatever he undertook, and in his helpfulness to his relatives and associates.

Pamphilus is a very important link between the third and fourth centuries, both theologically and textually. While in prison he wrote *An Apology for Origen*, which was completed by Eusebius (it is now lost, except for a Latin translation of Book 1). Textually, he clearly paid attention to the task of continuing Origen's work of establishing the text of the Septuagint. His library included the master copy of the Hexapla. A well-known quotation from Jerome's preface to his Latin translation of Chronicles (produced in 396) bears out his role:

the Palestinian provinces use the codices which Origen produced and Eusebius and Pamphilus made popular.

The second colophon is more informative. This is what it states: the corrector whom we call cpamph compared Codex Sinaiticus with a copy of the five books 1 and 2 Chronicles, 1 and 2 Esdras and Esther. This 'extremely old copy' had been made by two prisoners in Caesarea (at a time which we can establish to have been 307–09). It had been very carefully produced, Antoninus copying it and Pamphilus correcting it. The source from which they copied it was the master copy of the Hexapla, containing Origen's own corrections.

The corrections by cpamph would therefore be only one copying (two if we include the process of making the changes in Codex Sinaiticus) away from one of the most important stages in the development of the Greek Bible, namely Origen's Hexapla.

Moreover, the colophons make a connection with books whose location we know. Jerome writes in his book *On Famous Men* that

Pamphilus the presbyter, patron of Eusebius Bishop of Caesarea, burned with such love for the divine library, that he copied the majority of the works of Origen in his own hand; they may be found today in the library at Caesarea.

It may be that Jerome had seen them for himself. Such a collection would not be lent out: anyone who wanted to consult one of these works would have to go to the library. On the face of it, then, the colophon implies that Codex Sinaiticus was in Caesarea and actually in the library when this set of corrections was made.

This colophon locates an important link in the chain of passing down the text. As it happens, it combines with Eusebius' account to place the work in a highly charged environment of physical and psychological violence. No ivory tower for Pamphilus and Antoninus, these were textual scholars who also maintained their allegiance to the death.

Should we believe this claim? There are arguments both for and against it. In favour of it is the fact that there is evidence that the text given by cpamph is indeed similar to the form of the Septuagint known to Origen. Against it is the frequency with which a colophon making similar claims appears in very different texts and manuscripts of the Old and New Testaments.

Another difficulty is that the size of the codex described in the colophon is problematical. There is no evidence that Christians were producing parchment codices as early as about 310, when Pamphilus was in prison, and the circumstances under which he and Antoninus would have been working are such that everyday papyrus seems a more likely material to have been available. But no single papyrus codex could have contained so much text. The four books of Kingdoms, two books of Esdras and Esther are one third larger again than the largest papyrus codex of the New Testament. It is therefore more likely that there was at least one parchment intermediary manuscript, containing colophons carried over from earlier separate papyrus copies.

This possibility is supported by what is known about the history of the Caesarean library. Established by Origen, it was further developed by Pamphilus and Eusebius. After Eusebius, his successors Acacius and Euzoius seem to have concentrated on conservation, replacing papyrus books with parchment. If this restoration included copying Pamphilus' autographs, complete with colophons, then the copy available to later scholars will not have been identical with the original.

The later history is also relevant. The last person to refer to the library seems to have been Jerome, who died in 420. What eventually happened to it is unknown, but the history of Caesarea after the seventh century was one of decline. The city was held by the Persians between 614 and 628, and taken by the Arabs in 640/1. There is no evidence for extensive destruction (the archaeological record suggests little damage from the Persians and some from the Arabs). The library may have been dispersed, partly lost, and partly have mouldered away. What we can say is that all colophons in manuscripts copied from the eighth century onwards which claim descent from a Pamphilian source cannot be evidence of a direct link. What will have happened is that colophons will have been copied from one manuscript to another, so that we have a string of transmission, with a steadily dwindling similarity to the Pamphilian tradition, and even the possibility of the colophon becoming attached to a quite different text.

With regard to the Pamphilian corrections in Codex Sinaiticus, we can say that they are old enough comfortably to pre-date the destruction of the library. On the other hand, the colophon may be copied from a copy of a copy. That is, we have to be careful about the claim that Codex Sinaiticus must have been in Caesarea to have this material written in it.

Origen, Eusebius and Codex Sinaiticus

But it is worth pausing to consider one fact. Several names have come up regularly, notably Origen and Eusebius, and now the vital connection between them, Pamphilus. Why is this? One reason is that Origen and Eusebius were among the most important Christian writers of their age, in their thinking and their scholarship. Origen had a profound influence on the Septuagint. Eusebius' system provided a key to reading the Gospels together. It is inevitable that Codex Sinaiticus, which brings together the entire biblical tradition just after Eusebius' time, should show signs of a tradition moulded by them both. It also happens to be the case that Origen and Eusebius were both not only prolific writers, but prolific writers of whose works a substantial number have survived. Eusebius' historical works are among the most important writings for our knowledge of early Christianity. So a lot of what we see is through his eyes, and this includes his report of Origen and Pamphilus.

But this does not mean that Codex Sinaiticus is itself necessarily or directly linked to anything reported by Eusebius. This needs to be remembered when considering the Pamphilian corrections and their colophons. They are not certain evidence providing a connection between Codex Sinaiticus and the textual scholarship of Caesarea. They are another intriguing piece of evidence which casts light on the highest textual aspirations of late antiquity, but probably promises more than it can deliver.

WHAT THE CORRECTORS DID

Why correct a manuscript? Codex Sinaiticus was rather carefully checked against the exemplar by the copyists. Yet it contains many subsequent corrections. There are several reasons why a later user may have wanted to revise a manuscript. They are:

to correct mistakes made by the scribe

to change the presentation, for example by insertion of punctuation, changing styles in spelling, even changes to line breaks for easier reading

to change the text to make it conform to a different text from the one the scribe intended to produce

Correction of mistakes by the scribe

These may be placed in three classes:

supplying text accidentally omitted

removing text accidentally supplied

replacing the wrong word with the right word

Of these three, omissions are most obviously significant. It is a good general rule that scribes omitted text more than they duplicated it. This is certainly true of Codex Sinaiticus, in spite of the fourteen repeated pages of 1 Chronicles. The obvious reason is a psychological one: copying was quite tedious, and so one wanted to get to the end as quickly as possible: wishful thinking led one to believe one had copied a piece of text when one hadn't. One of the most common reasons for this is the repetition of similar series of letters, causing the scribe to look at and copy the first series, then to look back at the exemplar and carry on from the second series.

Job contains one of the longest corrections of missing text, in the bottom margin of Q71-F8r, consisting of sixteen verses, 187 words. The most likely explanation for this is that the scribe missed out a block of text in the exemplar, perhaps a column or a page. The omitted text seems too short for him to have turned over two pages at once.

Changes in presentation

Changes in presentation are generally part of the 'noise' of a manuscript tradition. Words tended to be written as they were pronounced, punctuation would be more important to a reader than to a scribe, and easier line breaks would be very desirable in Codex Sinaiticus, where the lines are so short.

Revision against a different copy

This is the most interesting type of correction to us, because it tells us something about a manuscript that no longer survives (the chances of both a manuscript and a copy used to correct it both surviving from antiquity are negligible). The best way to illustrate what happened is with an example.

CORRECTION BY THE PAMPHILIAN CORRECTOR

A single page with a striking number of corrections is Q36-F4r. At a glance, one can see a couple of dozen annotations of different kinds in the margins and between the columns. What could have led to this flurry of activity? The best way to understand it is to start with the text as it was first written. Here is the first column of the page as it left the scriptorium, with the paragraphs as they are presented in the Codex. The passage is 2 Esdras 21.15–22.1 (Nehemiah 11.15–12.1).

15 17   son of Ezerei and Mathaniah son of Maca and Iobeb [18] son of Samouei, two hundred and eighty-four.

19   And the gatekeepers, Akoub Telamein and their brethren, were one hundred and seventy-two.

22   And the overseer of the Levites son of Banei Ozei son of Asabeia son of Ameica from the sons of Asaph, the singers, in charge of the house of the work of God. [23] For there was a command from the king concerning them. [24] And Patheia son of Baseza was at the king's hand in every affair concerning the people. [25] And for the villages, with their fields, and from the sons of Judah lived in Kariathar and and in Jesou [27] and in Bersabee

31   And the sons of Benjamein from Gaba, Machamas,

36   And of the Levites certain divisions in Judah were joined to Benjamin.

22.1   And these are the priests & the Levites coming up with Zorobabel son of Salathiel, and Jeshua Seraia, Jermeia

And here is the first part of the same text as it was revised by the Pamphilian Corrector, with an attempt to show how the revision would fit onto the page if it were in English, with the additional text and altered words in bold and cancelled words struck through. The numbers and symbols are those provided by the corrector to help the reader through the text. The result is far from easy to decipher.

See Plate 9a

> **2**
>
> ·ɣ sons of Zechri, son of Asaf, overseer of the praise
> of Judah in prayer & Bakbakias
> second of his brethren & Abdas
> son of Sammoue, son of Galel, son of Idithoun.
> All the Levites in the holy city

> **1**
>
> ·ɣ son of Asabiou, son of Bonnai &
> Sobbathaios & Jozabad, over
> the exterior work of the house
> of God: from the leaders of the
> Levites

1

15 17   son of **Ezrikan** ·ɣ and **Math-**
thanias   **2**
son of Macas ·ɣ ~~and Iobeb~~
18   ~~son of Samoue~~i, two
hundred and eigh-
ty-four.
19   And the gatekeepers, Akoub
Telamein and their
brethren, ⁖̇ were one

> ⁖̇
> the kee-
> pers in
> the gates

hundred and seventy-   **3**
two. **The rest of Israel, the priests** ·ɣ
22   And the overseer of the Levites **in Jerusalem was Aza,**
son of Bonei ~~Ozei~~
son of Asabeia **son of Mathanios**
son of **Meica**
from the sons of Asaph,
the singers, in
charge **of the work of the**
23   **house** of God. For there was a command from the king con-
cerning them. | & it continued for the singers every day on the same day |
24   And **Phatheia** son of Ba-
beel, of the Zare son of Judah
seza was at the king's
hand in every
matter concerning the people.

Just by looking at the page, we learn one important thing: cpamph is concerned with textual accuracy, not with the ease of the reading experience (and it is hard to make sense of the expanded verse 24). This is a scholar's text.

Taking the whole column, nearly two hundred words have been supplied later. In fact, the scribe only wrote 152 words, so the final form of this column of text is twice as long as the original. This is a highly unusual example, but only in the degree of what we may observe, not in the nature of it.

On this page, the long lists of personal and place names, and the frequent repetition of the phrase 'and the villages thereof' gave the scribe good cause to believe that he was being more conscientious than was really the case. But here there seem to be deeper underlying causes. One is almost tempted to think that the scribe believed that in the case of 2 Esdras, less was better. Was this the state of the manuscript in the exemplar? Since there are only two scriptorium corrections on this page, it seems possible. Perhaps at some stage the text had been copied by a hardened professional who reckoned that the patron would never notice a short version of this passage.

WHY?

Why was Codex Sinaiticus corrected so much more fully than any other manuscript? And why was the Old Testament corrected more extensively than the New? The answer to the first question can only be speculative. My suggestion would be that it had already a sufficiently high status in the first centuries after its creation to be treated with extraordinary care. With regard to the higher degree of attention to the Old Testament, one has to differentiate between different books. 2 Esdras and Esther received very detailed scholarly attention. The prophetic books were not very well written in the first place, and therefore needed more work to get them up to standard. In addition, one may speculate that the Codex may have been in a setting where there were fewer copies of the Old Testament than of the New, and was therefore used more.

SOURCES AND FURTHER READING

The translation of the colophons to 2 Esdras and Esther is based on T. C. Skeat's in 'The Use of Dictation in Ancient Book-Production', *Proceedings of the British Academy* 42 (1956), pp. 179–208, reprinted in J. K. Elliott (ed.), *The Collected Biblical Writings of T. C. Skeat* (Novum Testamentum Supplement Series 113), Leiden and Boston, Mass.: E. J. Brill, 2004, pp. 3–32, p. 18.

For Eusebius' account of Pamphilus and the quotation describing his virtues, see *The Martyrs of Palestine* 11.1. There is a discussion of the archaeological evidence for the location of the prison in J. Patrich, 'The Urban Context for the Acts of the Martyrs of Caesarea', *Qatedrah le-tôldôt Eres Yisra'el el we-yîššûbah* 107 (2003), pp. 5–26.

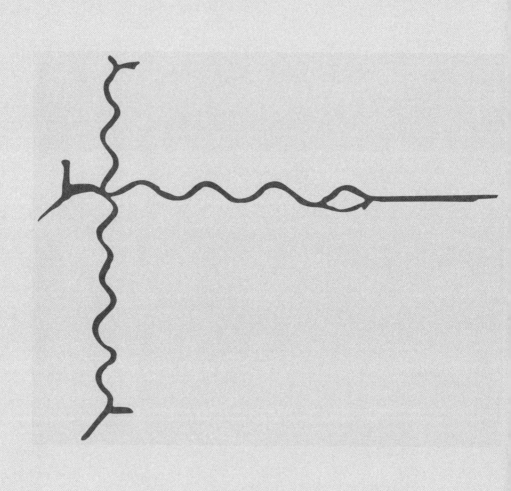

CHAPTER SEVEN

The Text of the Bible in
Codex Sinaiticus

C ODEX SINAITICUS is one of our most important ancient copies of the Bible. Editors of both the Septuagint and the New Testament, not to mention Barnabas and Hermas, frequently print a text similar to that found in Codex Sinaiticus. While the scribes may have varied in the accuracy of their copying, and while they had as their exemplars poorer copies of some books than of others, every editor will want to know what Codex Sinaiticus reads every time there is a decision to be made as to the older form of wording.

The manuscript has different roles to play in the editing of the two testaments and the two books at the end, and what follows will try to describe how these roles differ. Faced with thousands of differences of all kinds across the entire Bible, one can do no more than try to present a few of the most interesting examples.

THE OLD TESTAMENT

The nature of the differences between the Septuagint and the English versions have already been described. To sum them up, they consist of differences in the number and order of the books and differences in wording. In addition, distinctive wording of the Septuagint in Codex Sinaiticus makes the reading of the Old

Testament a very different experience from reading other forms of the Septuagint, let alone reading the Hebrew Massoretic Text.

Some of the distinctive features in Codex Sinaiticus are caused by the scribes, some are older. It is not always possible to tell how a particular wording arose, since we do not always know what the 'original' text of the Septuagint was. The situation is best explained by a discussion of examples.

Judges

The discovery of five sequential leaves from Judges, containing 4.7–11.2, was the largest block of text in the New Finds. For editors and students of the text of Judges, it offers an exciting opportunity to explore new material and reassess the history of the book. This will be done by a careful comparison of the wording of Codex Sinaiticus with that of other Greek copies. Judges is the most baffling example of a book in which two separate ancient Greek texts have survived. One is best attested in Codex Alexandrinus, and is called A. The other, known from Codex Vaticanus, is referred to as B. It seems likely that both are descended, through independent revisions, from the same original translation. Which does Codex Sinaiticus follow, or does it even throw the whole scheme into disarray? This will require a proper study on its own. But let this be the place where the problem is first studied. A glance at the Song of Deborah in Chapter Five (a notoriously difficult passage in the Hebrew) will give us a taste of what needs to be done (Q18-F3v-C4-L29 – F4r-C1-L11).

We must remember that we are studying a previously unknown copy of the book, so we must try to sit loose to all existing theories. A good way to begin is by comparing the text with that of Codex Vaticanus. If they are fairly similar, then we will immediately have an initial hypothesis that it too has the B text. If there are many differences, we will have to try comparing it with A instead. If there are still a lot of differences, then we will probably need a more sophisticated way of working.

In verses 2 and 3 the new text agrees precisely with the B text (except for a few spellings and a confusion). Then in verse 4 we find a difference. B reads 'heaven dripped dews'; Codex Sinaiticus reads 'heaven groaned'. Is this an agreement with the other form of text? No, because A reads 'heaven was shaken'. This is intriguing, but it is too early to start looking for explanations. We must go on comparing the texts. In verse 5 there is an addition in our new text: where B reads clumsily

The mountains were shaken before the face of the Lord Eloei, this of Sinai

Codex Sinaiticus has

The mountains were shaken before the face of the Lord Eloei, this of Sinai
Before the face of the God of Sinai

This looks like an explanation of the difficult phrase 'this of Sinai'. The next verse brings another explanation to what looked like a mistake in B. The Greek word for 'in' is *en*, and it seemed that the scribe of B had written the word twice after the name Anath: Anath en en. But Codex Sinaiticus has the same, so we must conclude that this is unlikely to be a mistake, and is more likely to be a variant of the proper name: Anathen.

The corrections in Codex Sinaiticus also provide new evidence. There is an excellent example in verse six. Here the B and A texts have quite different understandings of the Hebrew. According to B,

they left roads and took byways
they took winding roads

According to A,

she left kings and took paths
she took winding roads

Codex Sinaiticus agrees with B. But Corrector ca decided that the first 'roads' was wrong, and replaced it with 'kings', and cb2 subsequently inserted 'paths' before 'byways', so that the text ends up reading:

they left kings and took paths byways
they took winding roads

One can imagine that any copy of Codex Sinaiticus made after this point would have presented a confusion of the two versions. We can see the potential for new forms of the text to emerge.

The 'kings' of the A text is obviously in need of explanation. It has been suggested that it is a mistake in Codex Alexandrinus for another word meaning steps or foundations (*basileis* for *baseis*), only that would also be a strange translation of the Hebrew word, which means 'ways'. Perhaps the text is a confused attempt to translate the Hebrew as the royal highway.

There is much more work to be done, but this survey of the way its text enriches our understanding of a few new verses illustrates the impact that Codex Sinaiticus has had on research.

Esther

Esther is a prime example of the way in which the Greek and Hebrew differ. There are a number of places where the Hebrew text gives a summary which in the Greek is treated as an invitation to expand. And why should a storyteller not develop a tale? It is not only that there is more to the Greek Esther. The whole story has a different set of emphases. Esther is one of the two books of the Bible which do not contain the word 'God'; to be precise, Hebrew Esther does not contain the word. The Greek version makes up for that omission, notably in the concluding words put on the lips of Mordecai, which begin 'These things are the Lord's doing'. Likewise his prayer at the end of Chapter Four sets the whole tale in a more devout framework.

The additions were included by Jerome at the end of his translation of the Hebrew text, and so found their way into some English translations,

But the situation is a lot more complicated than a Hebrew text and a Greek text. Two ancient Greek versions of Esther have come down to us. The difference between the two versions may be illustrated from a famous phrase. In 1.19, we read of a royal decree 'among the laws of the Persians and the Medes, that it be not altered'. This is an important part of the story, for it means that later on the edict against the Jews cannot be rescinded. Instead, a second edict has to be issued giving the Jews permission to defend themselves. While the Septuagint contains the explanatory reference to the law of the Medes and the Persians in 1.19, it is lacking from the other version (known as the Alpha-Text). We do not need to discuss further issues relating to this Alpha-Text, whether it is derived from a different Hebrew text than the Septuagint, or whether it is wholly a revision of the Septuagint (some dependence upon it is agreed). Suffice it to say that Codex Sinaiticus belongs to the Septuagint version.

notably the Roman Catholic Douay-Rheims version (Old Testament published 1609–10). A convenient way to read the expanded version is in the Jerusalem Bible, which prints the Greek additions in italics.

Another important difference is that Esther herself plays a larger role. The insertion of her prayer in Chapter Four and the fuller psychological portrait of her appearance before the king in Chapter Five are the main contributors to this.

Tobit

This is another book to have survived in more than one Greek form. In fact three are known. Codex Sinaiticus is the only Greek witness to the second form. It is supported in it by the oldest translation into Latin. The spread of Christianity was initially through Greek-speaking areas and cities: the letters of Paul and the Acts of the Apostles make this clear enough. It is only in the course of the third century that evidence begins to emerge of translations into other languages. The three from this period about which we know are Syriac, Latin and Coptic. The oldest manuscript copies are none of them older than the third quarter of the fourth century, and in the case of Old Latin Tobit are four centuries after that. But the version tells us something about the long-lost Greek manuscript which the translator used. So we know that the translator of the Old Latin version of Tobit, made in the third or fourth century, used a Greek manuscript similar to Tobit as we know it in Codex Sinaiticus. This version seems to be the closest of the three to the underlying Semitic original.

Jeremiah

The Massoretic and Septuagintal forms of Jeremiah are very different, and in fact disagree even in the way the material is ordered. The work contains a number of blocks of text, which are generally divided into four thematic groups. In the Massoretic Text, the first (Chapters 1–25) consists of prophecies against Judah; the second (Chapters 26–45) contains for the most part oracles about the prophet himself; the third (Chapters 46–51) comprises prophecies against other nations, and the last (Chapter 52) is a historical account of Nebuchadnezzar's siege and capture of Jerusalem that is taken from 2 Kings 24.18–25.21. The Septuagint is witness that this is not the only form in which the text once circulated in Hebrew. Part Three (the prophecies against other nations) is placed near the end of Part One, after 25.14, and the constituent parts of it are reordered. The following table shows the order in the Septuagint, and therefore Codex Sinaiticus, against the Massoretic Text:

	Septuagint	Hebrew (and English) text
Elam	25.14–20	49.34–9
Egypt	26	46.2–28
Babylon	27–28	50–51
Philistines	29	47.1–7
Edom	30.1–16	49.7–22
Ammonites	30.17–21	49.1–6
Kedar	30.23–28	49.28–33
Damascus	30.29–33	49.23–7
Moab	31	48
Heading	32.13	46.1

Moreover, the two main editions of the Septuagint differ in their numbering. The chapter and verse numberings in Jeremiah are confusing!

Only with the final chapter do the chapter and verse numbers realign.

An equally striking difference is found in the length of the two books: the Septuagint contains about one-eighth less material (translating a Hebrew text containing 2,700 fewer words than the Massoretic Text). Sometimes the shorter text may be due to an omission at an earlier stage in the tradition. But sometimes it may be older than the Massoretic Text.

There are fragments of Hebrew manuscripts among the Dead Sea Scrolls which agree with the Septuagint against the Massoretic Text. This new evidence has led to a fresh assessment of the growth of Jeremiah.

The Psalter

Every user of Codex Sinaiticus needs to know that there is a difference in the numbering system between the Hebrew (and so the English) and the Greek. They agree as far as Psalm 8. But Psalms 9 and 10 in English are a single psalm in the Greek, so that English Psalm 11 is Greek Psalm 10 (and our Psalm 23 is Greek Psalm 22). Thus they run along the one ahead of the other until we reach our Psalm 147, which the Septuagint makes into two, so that verses 1–11 are Psalm 146 and 12–20 are Psalm 147. The next three numbers are the same, but the Septuagint has a Psalm 151.

The title indicates that Psalm 151 has a peculiar status: 'This is a psalm of David and does not have a number. When he overcame Goliath.' Although it for long seemed probable that it was composed in Greek, several fragments among the Dead Sea Scrolls look likely Hebrew prototypes, so we must reckon again that this is a place where the Hebrew from which the Septuagint Psalter was translated differed from the Massoretic Text.

The most striking features of this book in Codex Sinaiticus are graphically illustrated. The titles, which refer variously to author-ship, occasion and musical accompaniment, are in red ink. They often differ from the Hebrew headings. There are also occasional musical directions in which the two differ. For example, *diapsalma*, 'an interlude on strings', written in red in Codex Sinaiticus after 2.2 (Q59-F1r-C1-L26), is not present in the Hebrew. The frequency of the differences between Hebrew and Greek may be compared with the way in which the Syriac translation (which by the way contains 155 psalms) has its own very different set of rubrics. Where such a rubric gives a different setting to the psalm, the entire interpretation is at stake. This evidence suggests that the titles and musical directions were quite freely adapted to suit local views and tastes.

The other striking feature is the layout. The selection of a two-column format for the poetical books is due to the scribes' desire to do justice to the literary character of the works. The most important feature of Hebrew poetry is parallelism:

Lord, who shall abide in thy tabernacle?
who shall dwell in thy holy hill? (Psalm 15)

The very short fixed-length lines of the prose books would destroy this. The next section will show how scribes could be sensitive to the metrical quality of 1 Corinthians 13. They had the right idea here. But how successful was the result? Ideally, one would want to see each line of verse on its own. In fact, the columns are often still too short. We can see this at the very beginning:

Blessed is the man that walketh not in the coun-
   sel of the ungodly
nor standeth in the way of sinners (Q59-F1r-C1-L1-L3)

The scribe makes the best of it by indenting the text that has run over, but it is still a little disappointing. This was a common enough problem. Codex Alexandrinus, which always has two columns, struggles even more with the poetical structure. And a single column would have been prodigiously wasteful of materials.

THE NEW TESTAMENT IN CODEX SINAITICUS

The copying of the Septuagint was influenced by special circumstances (namely, that it was a translation from a Hebrew original, and that it circulated among both Jews and Christians) which do not apply to the New Testament writings. Since these were produced within various early Christian groups, and written in the language in which they are found in Codex Sinaiticus, we are dealing with different issues and problems.

There is another way in which we are in a different situation in studying the New Testament, namely in the far greater number of manuscripts available to us (something in excess of five and a half thousand copies, as was noted in Chapter Two). Of these, though, the great majority are Byzantine, and the number which contain older forms of the text is fairly small, even though there are more than for the Old Testament. As there, we have the other major Bible manuscripts, Vaticanus and Alexandrinus and Ephraemi Rescriptus in particular. We also have some sensational newer discoveries which have helped us to understand the text much better.

These discoveries are the result of the kind of searches which followed the age of Tischendorf. His was the era during which the majority of the surviving parchment manuscripts of the fourth century and onwards were discovered. In the following generation, as archaeologists began to find papyrus manuscripts in the desert sands of Egypt, even older copies began to come to light. The golden age of these discoveries lasted from about 1900 to the 1960s. There are now remains of over one hundred such papyri, the oldest written perhaps in the middle of the second century. They include New Testament verses written for magical purposes, to protect the user (in the case of amulets, the wearer) from evil, texts written for telling fortunes, and more literary productions, of which some are well written and careful. Of them, half a dozen stand out. They may even have belonged together in antiquity, though now they are separated. Three are among the Chester Beatty papyri, discovered and published in the 1930s and now in Dublin. Together they originally contained the Gospels and Acts, Paul's letters and Revelation. They date from the third century.

The other three belong among the Bodmer papyri, which were acquired by the Fondation Martin Bodmer in the 1950s, and were published from 1958 onwards. The oldest of these, containing the Gospel of John, was written in about 200. Another, of Luke and John, is almost as old, while the third, containing Jude, 1 and 2 Peter and other texts, dates from about 300.

Byzantine here means that they contain the form of text which was dominant from the seventh century onwards.

The Bodmer papyri were until 2007 all held in Geneva. In that year, the manuscript of Luke and John was sold to an organisation which then presented it to the Vatican Library.

These are not necessarily the oldest copies, but they are the most extensive and the most significant. They give us an insight into a period which before their discovery was even harder to understand than it is now. Until the 1930s, Codex Vaticanus and Codex Sinaiticus were still the oldest extensive copies of the New Testament. And we should remember that it was only in the nineteenth century that the former became widely known and the latter known at all.

The New Testament texts were written by authors living in the first century, and so for a scholar of 1900 there was a gap of nearly three hundred years between the authorship of the texts and the oldest copies. It was as though the oldest surviving copy of Shakespeare's plays dated from 1850. Where no older copies exist, we have to devise methods which will help us to decide what forms of text the older lost copies may have contained. Suppose that Codex Sinaiticus and Codex Vaticanus are the only two copies of the New Testament in existence, that there are no other manuscripts or printed editions in Greek or any other language. How do we reconstruct the text? Where they agree, there are two possibilities: either they are right or they are wrong. If they are right, then we have nothing more to think about. But if we think that they are both wrong, we will have to conjecture what we think is a better wording. Where they differ, there are three possibilities: either one of them is right, or neither is right. If we decide that neither can be right, then again we must conjecture what was the older lost wording. We can see examples of all these when we compare the two manuscripts.

Where they are both right consists of all those places where there is no reason to suspect any kind of alteration to the text. For example, at John 1.1 they both read 'In the beginning was the Word, and the Word was with God, and the Word was God', without a letter's difference between them.

An example where they are both wrong may be suggested at Matthew 27.49 (Q80-Fir-Ci-Li in Codex Sinaiticus). Here they include the words 'But another, taking a spear, pierced his side and there came out water and blood.' This verse is found in John (19.34), where the event happens after Jesus has died. Here it interrupts the story and seems to be an alternative cause of death. It is reasonable to suppose that the verse is a common feature, an intrusion of wording from one Gospel into another.

An example where Codex Vaticanus is right and Sinaiticus wrong is found at Luke 13.27 (Q80-F1r-C1-L1 in Codex Sinaiticus). In a parable, the direct speech of the householder begins in Codex Vaticanus as '. . . he will say, saying to you . . .'. In Codex Sinaiticus it reads '. . . he will say to you . . .'. The former is an awkward con-struction, but rather a common one in the Gospels, where one often finds phrases such as 'Answering he said . . .' One can understand why a later user might want to tidy it up.

An example where they differ and both are wrong is found at Romans 8.35. In Codex Sinaiticus (Q82-F4r-C4-L24-L26), Paul asks 'Who can separate us from the love of God?'; in Codex Vaticanus he asks, 'Who can separate us from the love of God in Christ Jesus our Lord?' The second form is a harmonisation to the wording of verse 39, where it is said that nothing 'can separate us from the love of God in Christ Jesus our Lord'. The text in Codex Sinaiticus is probably an independent shorter harmonisation to verse 39. Paul is most likely to have written 'Who can separate us from the love of Christ?'

These are examples of the possible situations were these the only two manuscripts of the New Testament. But they are not. At any place in the Gospels one will have upwards of fifteen hundred Greek manuscripts, and hundreds in every other part. Even these are a tiny proportion of all the copies that have ever existed. The intense debate which has surrounded their interpretation and the frequency of copying have often produced variation which is either very hard to unravel, or highly significant for the meaning of the passage, or both. Codex Sinaiticus is always a key witness, as the following examples will demonstrate.

The name given to the way in which the Gospels affect each other's wording is harmonisation.

Anger

The saying of Jesus about anger at Matthew 5.22 (Q74-F2v-C4-L41)

See Plate 9b

has come down to us in two forms. As it was originally written in Codex Sinaiticus, it read 'Whoever is angry with a brother shall be liable to judgement.' But the meaning of the passage was debated. Was any kind of anger forbidden? What about other sayings such as 'Be angry but sin not', or 'Let not the sun go down on your anger'? These and other questions led to the view that Jesus was condemning inappropriate anger, and this interpretation is found in the addition of the Greek word *eikē*, 'without cause'. The change left its mark on Codex Sinaiticus: Corrector cb2 added the word in the margin. The passage is an excellent example of the way in which debate about the meaning of passages led to alterations in the wording (in the view of the person making the change, this was only clarifying the evident sense). It also illustrates how a very small change can have a momentous effect on the meaning.

The quotations are from Ephesians 4.26, the first of them a citation of Psalm 4.5 in the Septuagint.

The lilies of the field

And why take ye thought for raiment? Consider the lilies of the field, how they grow; they toil not, neither do they spin (Matthew 6.28).

The same saying is found at Luke 12.27, in a slightly simpler form, namely 'Consider the lilies, how they neither spin nor weave', as well as in a second wording very similar to Matthew's. It is also found in a third form in another gospel, the Gospel of Thomas. This text, purporting to be sayings by Thomas the Twin (see John 11.16; 20.24), consists of a collection of sayings attributed to Jesus. It is known from a Coptic version surviving in one fourth-century manuscript and from a number of Greek fragments. There has been a great deal of debate in recent years about the Gospel's value in recovering sayings of Jesus. Where they have similar sayings, is it wholly dependent upon the four canonical Gospels? Where it has its own unique sayings, are any of them authentic? Some scholars believe that there was a collection of sayings used by both Matthew and Luke, and some of them think that Thomas may contain material drawn from it independently of Matthew and Luke.

The collection is known as Q (from the German *Quelle*, meaning 'source').

Some scholars, on the other hand, are more doubtful as to the age

104

of the distinctive sayings in Thomas (some are obviously later), while others dispute the existence of Q.

As it is stands now, Codex Sinaiticus (Q74-F3v-C4-L22-L25) reads 'How they grow; they toil not, neither do they spin'. This is the text as it left the scriptorium. It had been known since the edition of Tischendorf that Codex Sinaiticus contained a correction here, but nobody had been able to read what was first written. So little trace remains of it, that it may have been corrected while the ink was still wet. It was one of the Greek fragments of the Gospel of Thomas, copied in around the year 200, which offered a clue to its decipherment. The first editors of the fragment (it was published in 1904) reconstructed the text as 'Much better are you than lilies which grow nor spin'. But the first word was damaged, and the awkward Greek ('nor' without a preceding 'neither') suggested to T. C. Skeat that it might be better reconstructed as 'do not card nor spin'. This gave him the idea that Codex Sinaiticus might have something similar, and the application of ultraviolet light to the manuscript led to the discovery that Scribe A originally wrote:

Consider the lilies of the field, how they do not card, neither do they spin nor toil

In the midst of all the debate about the Gospel of Thomas, the discovery of such a reading in Codex Sinaiticus has led to yet more discussion.

What is the evidence?
First it should be explained that in Greek there is quite a close visual similarity between 'they grow' and 'they do not card':

ΑΥΞΑΝΟΥΣΙΝ
ΟΥ ΞΕΝΟΥΣΙΝ

This kind of confusion between words suggested by something in the context is common enough in manuscript copies. It is due to the process by which the scribe reads a word and then processes it mentally before writing it down. Several similar examples by Scribe

A have been noted. At Psalm 103.12 the text was written as:

By them the birds of the air have their habitation
They sing from amidst the feathers

'Feathers' translates the Greek *pterōn*. The correct text is 'rocks', which in Greek is *petrōn*. The error in Codex Sinaiticus is due to the similarity of the words combining with the association of ideas between birds and feathers. It is a kind of mistake which everyone makes at one time or another.

Has something similar happened in Matthew? Perhaps the association of ideas (spinning and carding) combined with an approximate similarity of appearance to produce what reads like an improvement in the text. One of the most striking things about the verse as it was first written in Codex Sinaiticus is that it produced a construction paralleling verse 26: the fowls of the air 'sow not, neither do they reap, nor gather into barns'. The lilies of the field 'do not card, neither do they spin nor toil'. In each case the subjects are described as not doing three things. To some, this is a recommendation in favour of the reading. But is it a little too mannered? Might the structure of verse 26 have been a third influence working secretly on the scribe? Perhaps a structural difference between the two verses is a more likely rhetorical device.

We know that this other wording in Luke was so early, because it was the form used by Marcion, a writer and editor of the text who died in about 160. It is also found in several other early witnesses in Syriac and Latin (often a sign of a very old reading).

One of the most interesting things about this problem is that Luke also contains similar versions, 'Consider the lilies, how they neither spin nor weave' and 'Consider the lilies, how they grow; they neither toil nor spin'. The simplest explanation is that one form of the saying in Matthew ('Consider the lilies of the field, how they grow; they toil not, neither do they spin') was used by Luke, who simplified it to 'Consider the lilies, how they grow; they neither toil nor spin'. In the second century, a different Lukan form appeared: 'Consider the lilies, how they neither spin nor weave.'

Whether the Greek Gospel of Thomas contained 'how they grow' or 'how they do not card' cannot be determined because there is a hole in it. Given the tendency of Scribe A of Codex Sinaiticus occasionally to produce new versions of the text – and given the fact that Scribe D corrected the text to the form as it is found in other manuscripts, we cannot be sure that Scribe A is evidence for a variant form of the text. In short, 'they do not card' may occur only in Codex Sinaiticus, and there only as a piece of confusion by Scribe A. It is also possible that the scribe knew this form from another source, was perhaps more familiar with it than with what was in his exemplar, and wrote it without thinking, then the corrector realised it was wrong, and copied the exemplar's text. Either way, the form 'do not card' is more likely to be an 'improvement' – caused by similarity of letters and the context – than the oldest form of the text.

The story has all the glamour of modern scholarship: an ancient fragmentary copy of an apocryphal Gospel; a reading in a Gospel codex recovered by modern technology; and a suggestion that the two may combine to give us access to a very ancient form of a saying of Jesus in a supposedly very early Christian document. But there is more glamour than substance. We may continue to consider the lilies of the field, how they grow.

Rediscovering St Mark's Gospel

The story of biblical research in the past two hundred years has been the story of the recovery of older forms of the text. After many centuries during which the text had always evolved from the previous stage to a new one, the early nineteenth-century editors began to work back the other way, making a new stage of the text by going back hundreds of years to the oldest copies. There is an analogy with period performance of baroque music. The manufacture of instruments and editions of texts having evolved stage by stage (from the harpsichord to the fortepiano to the pianoforte to the modern concert grand), instrument makers and editors went back to original sources and tried to cut out the intervening developments, imitating surviving seventeenth-century harpsichords and using the manuscript scores as the basis for performance. In the same way textual editing abandoned the point which had been reached in favour of imitating the oldest available resources.

In the case of the Gospel of Mark, the return to ancient forms of the text was startling, because it revealed a book that had been obscured by later additions.

To start with, the beginning had been adapted. Read the Authorised Version and it starts: 'The beginning of the Gospel of Jesus Christ, the Son of God.' These strong words are followed by a dramatic plunge straight into the story, with the description of John baptising and Jesus' baptism by him, concluding with heavenly words vindicating the opening: 'Thou art my beloved Son, in whom I am well pleased.'

The beginning in Codex Sinaiticus was (originally) different. Here the first sentence is: 'The beginning of the Gospel of Jesus Christ.' Again it is followed by the story of John the Baptist, and the same words from heaven. But now these words have a different sound to them, for Jesus Christ is being addressed as the Son for the first time. To some early Christians, Jesus was made Son of God at his baptism, and this is probably what Mark intended. In later generations, and especially in controversies in the third and fourth centuries about such topics, the idea that Jesus was 'adopted' as God's Son, rather than having always been so, was increasingly regarded as inadequate. There were richer ideas in the concept of his eternal sonship. Thus it may have been that Mark's understanding of the matter was later clarified by the insertion of the words 'the Son of God' in verse 1.

See Plate 9c

But the story is a little more complicated than that. For Codex Sinaiticus left the scriptorium with the missing two words added (see Q76-F2v-C1-L2) above the line. Thus, the scribe who added them (was it A, was it D?) knew both forms of text. It is unlikely that the shorter form can have been accidental, since it seems odd for a scribe to make such a mistake in the second line of copying a text. Moreover, the verse is found without the words in other sources, notably a few manuscripts (not Codex Vaticanus, which contains them) and quotations in two early Christian writers: Irenaeus, Bishop of Lyons between 178 and 200, and Origen. Did the scribe know the shorter form in his head, and then when checking the manuscript against his exemplar realise he had omitted words present in it, and supplied them? Was the absence of the words noticed in some other way? To be fanciful, did a visitor walk into the scriptorium, glance at a few sheets, and suggest that other copies read 'son of God' at the beginning of Mark?

Codex Sinaiticus is a perfect witness to the fact that the words still had an uncertain place in the text. By the fifth century, they had become fully established.

Throughout the Gospel of Mark, the text came frequently to be altered to conform with the wording of the other Gospels. While today it is recognised as the oldest of them, the church fathers believed that it was dependent upon Matthew and, because almost all of Mark's Gospel was used by Matthew, it was easy to harmonise it in the direction of Matthew. This process of incremental harmonisation was so universal that it only came to be recognised when older manuscripts were found and studied, and the varnish of later embellishments removed to reveal the original colourings of Mark's book.

Perhaps the most dramatic difference is found in the ending. Mark as it is given in Codex Sinaiticus (Q77-F5r-C1 bottom to C2) and Codex Vaticanus ends at 16.8: the women go to the tomb; it is empty and a young man tells them 'he is not here, he is risen' and that they will see him in Galilee; they flee the tomb, 'for they trembled and were amazed. They said nothing to anyone, for they were afraid.' No resurrection appearances, no mountain-top encounters with the risen Lord. By contrast, Matthew's Gospel, which used Mark's framework and developed it, includes an encounter with Jesus in the garden and the meeting in Galilee promised in Mark. Luke, coming third, includes other stories, notably the story of the journey to Emmaus and the meeting in the upper room, and John adds yet more.

It seems that Mark's version came to seem inadequate compared to the other three, and various endings were provided that better did justice to the tradition. One is a coda to verse 8. Another is a summary of resurrection appearances from other Gospels (verses 9–20).

The view that led to harmonisation was the view that the four Gospels were slightly differing versions of a single overarching story. Today there is more interest in reading the four Gospels as texts that provide four different insights into the emergence of Christianity. The different textual forms of each Gospel provide further information about the ways in which the texts continued to be changed as Christian thought and life developed. Thus, the form of Mark in Codex Sinaiticus (catching the transition in form of the very first verse, containing a good deal of harmonisation and ending at 16.8) is a snapshot of the tradition, a form of the text as Scribe A reproduced it in the middle of the fourth century.

The story of the woman taken in adultery

One of the most popular of all the stories in the Gospels, this event (found in most manuscripts at John 7.53–8.11) is missing from the oldest manuscripts, including Codex Sinaiticus. What are we to make of this? The short answer is that there is no convincing reason why anybody should choose to omit it, but every reason why such a story, once it became popular, should get added. It seems to have become known as a story about Jesus in the course of the second century, but the oldest manuscript to contain it (Codex Bezae) was copied in around the year 400. It is the most striking example of a popular story finding its way into the Gospels long after their composition. It was inserted at this place in this Gospel because it uses a break in the narrative shortly before Jesus says (8.15) 'I pass judgement on no one'. The story therefore provides an event giving rise to a discourse by Jesus, just as the feeding of the five thousand (Chapter 6) leads to the discourse 'I am the bread of life', as the healing of the man born blind culminates in Jesus' proclamation that he has come 'to give sight to the sightless and to make blind those who see' (9.39), and as the raising of Lazarus includes the words 'I am the resurrection and the life' (11.25). The addition of the story before 8.12 provides the same device of using a narrative as the prologue to a discourse.

The story is interesting, not only in itself, but because it reveals that pieces of text were being added to the Gospels even in the late fourth century onwards. The written Gospels were not treated as fixed entities to be revered as they have come to be in some quarters, especially since the Protestant Reformation. They were regarded as witnesses to the tradition, as part of the collection of beliefs and ways of life that made Christianity what it was. To include an accepted part of the tradition in the Gospel was not to tamper with it, but to ensure that it did not have less than the richness of the entire tradition.

John 21

Codex Sinaiticus itself, the facsimile and the digital images all look perfectly normal in Q81-F6r-C4. But Tischendorf suspected that there was something odd about the last few lines of John's Gospel. He decided that the scribe stopped dead at the end of verse 24, without adding the usual coronis and subscription. He thought that verse 25 was lacking in the exemplar, and was added by Scribe D, along with the coronis and subscription. His grounds were a difference in ink colour, and a supposed difference in the hand. Other scholars, including Lake, thought that the change in colour was due to the scribe taking a fresh dip in the ink pot. To resolve the problem, Milne and Skeat gave the page a strong dose of ultraviolet light. They saw that what had happened was that the scribe ended John prematurely and wrote the subscription and coronis. Realising his mistake he washed out the subscription and coronis, copied the missing verse 25, and then rewrote them. Washing ink off as effectively as it has been done here has to come soon after the writing, and it is far more likely that this was a casual mistake (wanting to get

Ultraviolet light of a level considered acceptable today shows nothing beyond what is visible to the naked eye.

to the end?) on the scribe's part, and that the last verse was present in the exemplar, rather than that this is our only evidence for a version of John which lacked the last verse.

1 Corinthians 13

See Plate 10

In this memorable passage, the scribe has given up writing with a fixed right margin and words broken across lines, and instead is writing in sense units. This has already started to happen in the second column, from 12.28. In verses 4 to 7 the text is broken into short phrases or single words:

Love
   is patient
   is kind
   love
   envies not
   love
   is not boastful
   is not puffed up
   is not rude
   seeks not her own
   is not easily provoked
   thinks no evil
   rejoices not in ini-
   quity · but rejoices
   in the truth
   bears all things
   believes all things
   hopes all things
Love ne-
   ver fails

This is not the only place where the scribe writes the text like this, but it is interesting that he should have chosen to do so in a passage with such a strong hymn-like quality. A few lines earlier, he gives a good example of his ability to omit: verses 1 to 2 read

If I speak in the tongues of men and of angels, but have not love, I am nothing.

The words are supplied by Scribe D in the top margin. The reason for this mistake is very simple: the words

ΑΓΑΠΗΝ ΔΕ ΜΗ ΕΧΩ ('but have not love')

come twice, in verse 1 and verse 2. Having read and written the first occurrence, the scribe looked back to his exemplar and copied on from the second one.

Verse 3 contains an interesting variation from the best-known English forms of the text, in which we read 'if I deliver my body to be burned'. The Greek word for 'burned', found in the later manuscripts, is ΚΑΥΘΗCΟΜΑΙ. But Codex Sinaiticus, along with the oldest manuscript and several other very important witnesses, reads ΚΑΥΧΗCΟΜΑΙ, 'if I give my body over for boasting'. This may sound strange. But there are good reasons why it is more likely to be what the Apostle wrote. First, there is no reason why in the 50s Paul would have believed that being a Christian could result in being burned to death. Such things were to come later. Second, Paul does talk about boasting quite a lot in this letter and in 2 Corinthians. It seems that the Corinthians had an opinion on it of which Paul did not approve. In both letters he quotes Jeremiah 9.23, 'Let him who boasts, boast in the Lord' (1 Corinthians 1.31; 2 Corinthians 10.17), and uses the term sarcastically ('so that I too may boast a little', 2 Corinthians 11.16). So here in 1 Corinthians 13 he is stating that even if one is so careless of one's body for one's beliefs as to be able afterwards to boast of the matter, this is nothing without love. The rule 'the harder reading is the better one' fits the case. In later times, when Christians *had* been burned for their faith, and when the details of Paul's disagreement with the Corinthians had been forgotten, the burning seemed the obvious reading. And again, we find that the only form of text available to the sixteenth-century editors and translators was this. Only recently did the ancient reading become known again.

These are a few instances of the ways in which reading Codex Sinaiticus is different from other experiences of reading the New Testament. There are many more places which would be interesting to discuss, but these examples illustrate some of the typical characteristics of a manuscript of the New Testament, especially one of that age. Of these, one may single out the evidence that the text was continuing to develop, even to the extent that Codex Sinaiticus did not include passages which would become well-known parts of the New Testament. One should also emphasise how as a manuscript copy it was unique: in otherwise unknown readings such as the lilies of the field; in the interplay of original text and correction such as the permission of reasonable anger and the beginning of Mark's Gospel; in errors such as the omission of a few words; and in the layout which presents the Hymn to Love in a unique format.

All these features are normal for a manuscript tradition, and are a part of the riches of the textual world until the Renaissance. By contrast, the print era, consisting as it does of widely accepted identical editions of texts, is one of textual poverty.

SOURCES AND FURTHER READING

For a general introduction to the Septuagint, see K. Jobes and M. Silva, *Invitation to the Septuagint*, Carlisle: Paternoster Press, 2001.

A lively introduction to the issues of textual variation in the New Testament is B. D. Ehrman, *Misquoting Jesus. The Story behind who Changed the Bible and Why*, New York: HarperCollins, 2005, published in the UK as *Whose Word is it Anyway? The Story* etc., London: Continuum, 2006. My book *The Living Text of the Gospels*, Cambridge: Cambridge University Press, 1997, also provides an introduction to textual criticism. The endings of Mark and the story of the woman are among passages discussed in more detail. See also J. K. Elliott and I. Moir, *Manuscripts and the Text of the New Testament. An Introduction for English Readers*, London and New York: Continuum, 1995.

The lilies of the field is discussed by T. C. Skeat, 'The Lilies of the Field', *Zeitschrift für die neutestamentliche Wissenschaft* 37 (1938), pp. 211–14 (reprinted in J. K. Elliott (ed.), *The Collected Biblical Writings of T. C. Skeat* (Novum Testamentum Supplement Series 113), Leiden and Boston, Mass.: E. J. Brill, 2004, pp. 243–46). See further Dirk Jongkind, '"The Lilies of the Field" Reconsidered: Codex Sinaiticus and the Gospel of Thomas', *Novum Testamentum* 48 (2006), pp. 209–16. The Gospel of Thomas may be read in J. K. Elliott, *The Apocryphal New Testament. A Collection of Apocryphal Christian Literature in an English Translation*, Oxford: Clarendon Press, 1993.

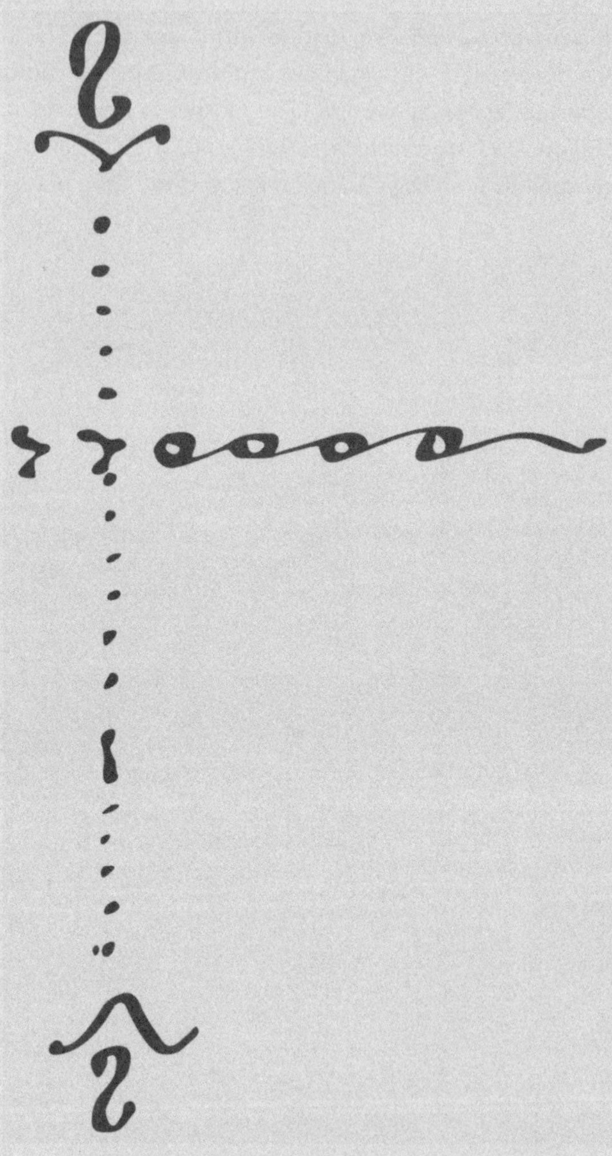

CHAPTER EIGHT

Beyond the Scriptorium

THE ANNOTATORS

SOME manuscripts suffer more heavily than others from annotations: jottings, doodles, sketches, pen trials, drafts of letters, records of business deals (the Lichfield Gospels record that someone acquired them in exchange for a very good horse). Codex Sinaiticus has got off very lightly. In one way this is disappointing: we learn less than we might otherwise have done about the history of the manuscript. But at any rate it remains on the whole what it began as – a majestic vehicle of the biblical text.

Dionysius

One of the few people to leave a record was a monk called Dionysius. He wrote three notes, on Q39-F3r, 66-6r and 66-7r. The first is a prayer, 'Remember Lord the soul of the sinner Dionysius the monk when you come in your kingdom.' The second is just his name. The third reads 'Remember Lord the monk Dionysius, a sinner'. Such jottings are often difficult to date very accurately, because they are written informally. Milne and Skeat hedged their bets by writing that 'the latest desultory scribblings to which any approximate date can be assigned seem to belong to the twelfth century'.

Theophylact

Another Byzantine reader left a longer note. It runs across the bottom of the opening Q68-Frv/2r, and appropriately beneath the words 'Wisdom's garland is the fear of the Lord' (Sirach 1.11): 'The bestower of all wisdom, Son of God and Word, the incarnate Wisdom of the Father who teaches knowledge to man, instruct the sinner Theophylact to the glory of your name that he may do your will.' A date around 1200 seems a safe proposal.

Notes of this kind are not at all uncommon in Byzantine manuscripts, though Dionysius' simple prayer is more typical than Theophylact's florid phraseology.

Theophylact also wrote a note at the bottom of Q72-F8v, and one Hilarion just wrote his name on Q42-F8v.

The Arabic glosses

Two people wrote comments here and there in the margins of the manuscript. For convenience we have named them Arabic A and Arabic B.

Arabic A wrote eight notes, seven of them against verses in Isaiah. The first is typical. On Q43-F1r-C1-L20, against Isaiah 1.10 ('Hear the Word of the Lord, you rulers of Sodom'), he wrote the explanation 'The Prophet rebukes the leaders of Israel'. The annotator seems to have been someone who knew Greek but also needed to write explanations of the content in Arabic (explaining that the address is to the leaders not of Sodom but of Israel). On Q58-F4v, below Column 4, he wrote with regard to Zechariah 14.8 'And from here it is required to explain'. There is no evidence assisting one to date the hand.

Arabic B's four notes are all in the margins of Revelation. At Q89-F3v, below Column 3 there is a note to 7.4 ('And I heard the number of those who were sealed, one hundred and forty thousand, sealed out of every tribe of the people of Judah'): 'One hundred and forty thousand believers who were marked with a seal – from the 12 tribes of Israel.' This is an accurate comment on the text as it is found in Codex Sinaiticus – almost every other manuscript reads 'one hundred and forty-*four* thousand'. Another note provides a date before which the note must have been written. Across the bottom of Q90-F4r, probably annotating 8.1 onwards, is a long comment explaining the prophecy of the seventh seal ([. . .] indicates un-readable text):

And at the beginning of the seventh thousand a persecution [of Christians] will take place. They say that [other] martyrs, who were martyred on the Messiah's lance [. . .] Then the peace and calmness will come and the number of holy men increase. Their [. . .] will be elevated and will compel them to appear in front of the Lord. And as a consequence will appear then a star of the Arabs, which looks like hellebore, will appear [. . .] This star is called afsintīs, which is absinth. It will fall into the water and many [. . .]

The seventh thousand is probably a reference to the date in the Byzantine calendar, which would be 1491 CE. The word afsintīs is a colloquial form, which may be associated with the Near Eastern drug trade. The spelling suggests that the writer was a Syrian.

Predictions that the world would end seven thousand years after its creation (1492 in the common reckoning) were made in the years after the fall of Constantinople in 1453. The first Patriarch under Ottoman rule, Gennadios II Scholarios, foretold that it would come on 1 September. This explains the glossator's interest in the Apocalypse, and gives an approximate date (after 1453 and before 1492) for the gloss.

THE MANUSCRIPT IN THE MIDDLE AGES AND BEYOND

The Arabic glosses are, unfortunately, the only evidence for the six hundred years between the twelfth-century glosses and the middle of the eighteenth century. It is highly probable that the Codex was in St Catherine's Monastery throughout the period. There is certainly no evidence to the contrary, and the presence of native Arabic speakers there is perfectly natural.

From the ninth century, the change in Greek script from majuscule to minuscule meant that fewer and fewer people were able to read the older scripts, until at last manuscripts like the Codex became useless. It was common enough for the parchment to be scraped down and reused (as was the case with Codex Ephraemi

Rescriptus). From this point on, Codex Sinaiticus is unlikely to have been used regularly.

The monastery library

From inscriptions on walls in the monastery, it is clear that before 1734 the books and manuscripts of St Catherine's were held in three different places. Texts of the services would have been kept in a room adjacent to the church. Books to be read by the community were in a central location, convenient for borrowing and returning. The oldest manuscripts were kept in a room in one of the towers. In fact this was the Tower of Saint George, in which the New Finds were discovered.

The situation changed when Archbishop Nikephoros Marthalis gathered all the books into one central location in 1734, in rooms opposite the archbishop's quarters. These arrangements continued until the books were transferred to the present library building in 1951. At the same time, there is evidence of another location: a description of 1817 refers to 'a second library of valuable books'.

An eighteenth-century visitor

It needed someone like the art historian and bibliographer Seymour de Ricci to find a reference to Codex Sinaiticus in the diary of an eighteenth-century Italian natural philosopher. Vitaliano Donati, famed for his *Della storia naturale marina dell'Adriatico* (1745), visited St Catherine's Monastery in 1761. His diary records that he was shown 'a Bible with very beautiful parchment folios, exceptionally large, fine and square, written in a round and very beautiful hand'. The temptation to identify this manuscript as Codex Sinaiticus is very strong. The description fits it more accurately than any other manuscript known to have been in the monastery (the shape being the most suggestive part of the description). Donati reports that of the large number of parchment codices he was shown, 'many are in a bookcase, others are lying around in a very unsatisfactory storeroom'.

Another possible sighting and a projected visit

The British officer Major Charles Kerr Macdonald visited Sinai in April 1845 in order to assess the region's turquoise deposits, with a view to their exploitation. He was also a collector, presenting the objects he found to the British Museum. It is recorded that he was shown a very old manuscript, which he thought was fourth century. There is currently only reported evidence concerning his visit, and it has been suggested that the source was oral.

In 1847, George Borrow was living in Oulton Broad in Suffolk and writing *Lavengro* and *Romany Rye*. His travels in Spain on behalf of the British and Foreign Bible Society were seven years and more in the past. What was to be his last adventure, to Constantinople, had been in 1844. In 1847, he became involved in plans by the British Museum for a visit to St Catherine's and elsewhere in search of manuscripts. Borrow was, as ever, keen on the idea of travel. But the scheme did not materialise. A correspondent wrote, in sounding him out on his interest, that among several manuscripts worth acquiring was 'an original copy of the Greek New Testament, said to be of the fourth century, that was presented to the Convent on Mount Sinai by the Emperor Justinian'. The significance of this story will become evident in the next chapter.

USE OF THE MANUSCRIPT IN THE EIGHTEENTH AND EARLY NINETEENTH CENTURIES

At some point, Codex Sinaiticus ceased to be complete. It lost most of its first thirty-four quires, and some also from the other end, along with a block of seven halfway through. There is evidence that the reason for at least some of this loss was the recycling of parchment in bookbinding. Several of the fragments in St Petersburg were taken from the bindings of manuscripts in the monastery library. Some pieces among the New Finds were cut in a shape which suggests that they were going to be used for the same purpose. Another whole leaf has folds which indicate that it was used as a dust

See Plate 11

The strength and suppleness of parchment makes it ideal for use in reinforcing spines.

jacket. Tischendorf was to find a small fragment being used as a bookmark (this was on his second visit, in 1853, an event to be described in Chapter Nine). There is also evidence of bookbinding having been carried on in the monastery. A number of tools for stamping bindings have been found. Apart from the interest of the tools themselves (they are very rare), it provides a way of identifying books from St Catherine's. Unfortunately, it is harder to associate these tools with binding operations involving pieces of Codex Sinaiticus, since some of them date from the sixteenth century and some from the mid-eighteenth.

The evidence from the New Finds sheds further light on these events. A part of the leaf containing Genesis 23 and 24 was among the pieces taken by Uspenski to St Petersburg in the 1840s. A piece of the previous leaf is among the New Finds. Likewise, a fragment from Quire 11 is in St Petersburg, while parts of Quires 10 and 12 are among the New Finds. What Uspenski took to St Petersburg, and what were subsequently found in bindings, were from quires, or leaves close to quires, which were placed in a room in the monastery, perhaps shortly after his visit.

The binding

The battered state of the last leaves of Hermas is an indication that the manuscript had been for some time without its covers, and this theory may be supported by the evidence of the stitching. The manuscript appears to have had two bindings in its history. The first was at its creation. The second was in comparatively recent times. Separately, the five leaves from Judges among the New Finds have at some point been 'overcast', stitched together in the way that today one would join a few sheets with staples down the left edge.

To make sense of all this, we must leap ahead in the story to 1975.

THE NEW FINDS

The discovery of 'new' manuscripts is always exciting, and the reality generally lives up to the first announcement. The opening of a room in St Catherine's in 1975 led to a dramatic discovery of a mass of manuscripts, leaves and fragments, comprising some or all of at least 1,100 manuscripts. About a third were complete codices. There were also more than 120 rolls, and very many leaves and fragments. These have proved to include the oldest Arabic Gospels, Greek biblical copies, and twenty-four leaves of Codex Sinaiticus, with forty fragments. Important for other reasons were new texts in the little understood Caucasian Albanian language.

See Plate 12

The finds include pieces used for bookbinding, so we know that Codex Sinaiticus was not the only manuscript treated in this manner. It also included fragments of baskets (the significance of which will appear in the next chapter).

It is possible that these materials were codices and pieces of codices and scrolls not removed to the new library in 1734. If so, we now have a plausible point by which Codex Sinaiticus had become dismembered. The presence of contemporary bookbinding tools; the use of leaves in bookbinding; the abandonment of parts of the book in the Tower of St George: all suggest an early eighteenth-century date for this.

Does the gap in the middle of the codex between Quires 50 and 56 suggest that the manuscript was originally bound in the Byzantine style, which would tend to break in the middle, the ends of both sections subsequently being lost?

But some evidence contradicts the theory. Donati may have admired the manuscript (though whether he saw it in the bookcase or the unsuitable storeroom we do not know). Most significant is the fact that Tischendorf and Uspenski, on the visits to be chronicled in the next chapter, were to see materials adjacent to some of the leaves in the New Finds. This undoubtedly suggests that the materials found in 1975 and those studied since the nineteenth century were not completely separated even in the 1840s. It is probably safest to conclude that the room of the New Finds was not completely forgotten, but that there was some flow of materials in and out in the early nineteenth century.

The story therefore seems to be one of the manuscript being preserved complete (or virtually so) until the eighteenth century. At that point the first thirty-four quires, a block of seven in the middle and the last three were separated from the rest and are now largely missing.

SOURCES AND FURTHER READING

The quotation from Milne and Skeat's *Scribes and Correctors* may be found on page 81.

I am indebted for information about the Arabic glosses to the report by Dr Nikolaj Serikoff, Asian Collections Librarian at the Wellcome Library, and to the comments of my colleague Professor David Thomas.

Donati's diary was edited by G. Lumbroso, *Ricerche Alessandrine,* in *Atti della Reale Accademia dei Lincei,* serie III. *Memorie della classe di scienze morali,* Vol. 4, 1879. I have not been able to find a copy of this volume. The diary itself is in the British Library (Ac. 102/3). I have been no more successful in tracking down De Ricci's article, which was published in *Revue archéologique* 14 (1909), p. 159. My source of information is H. J. M. Milne and T. C. Skeat, *The Codex Sinaiticus and the Codex Alexandrinus,* London: British Museum, 2nd edition, 1955, p. 5, note 1, and Professor Christfried Böttrich's account of the history of the manuscript written for the Project. It is to the latter that I owe the information about Major Macdonald, which is to be found in a note by S. P. Tregelles, who made an important edition of the Greek New Testament, in his Additions to T. H. Horne, *An Introduction to the Critical Study and Knowledge of the Holy Scriptures,* Vol. 4, 11th edition, London, 1863, p. 775. It is to Professor Böttrich also that I owe the quotation from the letter to Borrow, which may be found in W. I. Knapp, *Life, Writings and Correspondence of George Borrow (1802–1881),* Vol. 2, New York and London: John Murray, 1899, pp. 57–59.

For bookbinding at St Catherine's, see Nicholas Sarris, 'The Discovery of Original Bookbinding Finishing Tools at the Monastery of Saint Catherine', *Sinaiticus. The Bulletin of the Saint Catherine Foundation,* 2008, pp. 12–13.

There is an account of the New Finds in P. Nikolopoulos, 'The Library', pp. 349–55 of the magnificent K. A. Manafis (ed.), *Sinai: Treasures of the Monastery of Saint Catherine,* Athens: Ekdotike Athenon, 1990. See also the catalogue *The New Finds of Sinai,* Athens: Ministry of Culture and Mount Sinai Foundation, 1999.

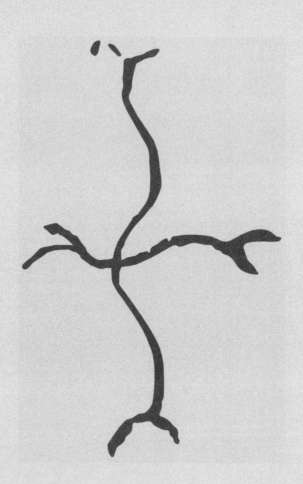

CHAPTER NINE

1844–1869

THE modern history of Codex Sinaiticus is inextricably linked to one person, namely Constantin von Tischendorf, variously described as scholar, editor of the Greek New Testament and explorer. The last runs the risk of exaggeration. He was not a Livingstone or a Burton. But he was a great traveller, always in search of manuscripts, which he would study for what they revealed about the text of the Bible. From the beginning, he recognised the value of making complete transcriptions of entire manuscripts, rather than listing the differences between them and other texts. In his day this was done by copying them by hand, setting them in type and then printing them. His earliest journeys were in southern Germany and Switzerland. Then he visited the extensive holdings of the Bibliothèque Nationale in Paris from 1840 to 1843, with subsidiary excursions to England and the Netherlands. A major achievement of this period was his transcription of the Codex Ephraemi Rescriptus (one of the ancient Bibles described in Chapter Two). Then he went on to Italy, sailing east in 1844 to Egypt. It was on this occasion that he first visited St Catherine's. The following years saw him marrying, settling down to professorial life in Leipzig, and publishing the fruits of his travels. These included transcriptions of another Parisian manuscript called Codex Claro-montanus (a sixth-century copy of Paul's letters containing the text in both Greek and Latin) and Codex Amiatinus, the great Vulgate Bible which had been copied in Bede's monastery in north-east England in the last decade of the seventh century. He also published his first editions of the Septuagint and of the Greek New Testament, and wrote an account of his travels. Two further journeys to St Catherine's followed, in 1853 and 1859. He published many further transcriptions and editions, most notably the eighth edition of his Greek New Testament, published in two volumes in 1869 and 1872. This remains one of the most comprehensive and accurate editions, and sets the gold standard for such work. Tischendorf also published a collection of poems in his student days. He was a neighbour and friend in Leipzig of both Robert Schumann and Felix Mendelssohn, the latter setting one of his poems to music.

But the concept is identical to that which lies behind the electronic transcription of Codex Sinaiticus (see Chapter 12).

For these connections see the website by Tischendorf's great-great-grand-nephew, at http://www.burg mueller.com/tisch endorf_e.html

THE VISIT OF 1844

The first trip to the East, and in particular the visit to St Catherine's, was a far bolder expedition than his European travels. The description by his son-in-law has the air of tales told by the family fireside in later years: the twelve-day journey across the desert by the scholar, the dragoman who acted as interpreter, three Bedouin and four camels (did one of them really have to walk?); the beauty of the desert night ('Above him the starry heavens of the East shone in incredible glory, and the camels grunted in the distance'). The trip was not without incident. 'A sudden breeze, which blew across from the Red Sea, carried off his straw hat . . . The three Bedouin chased after it, but returned after three-quarters of an hour without having retrieved it. Without a hat, however, the journey could not be continued, so back they went once more and searched all night, until by eight o'clock next morning they came back with it' (p. 39f).

A dragoman was an official interpreter of the Ottoman Empire.

The story of the twenty-nine-year-old Tischendorf's first encounter with the Codex is often told in his own words, without any attempt to evaluate them. It is sometimes even stated that he 'discovered' it: a plainly ridiculous verb, since it was already known and had long been known to the monks of St Catherine's. The most that can be said is that he was the first modern western scholar to study it.

See Plate 13

Tischendorf's account runs as follows:

I perceived in the middle of the great hall a large and wide basket full of old parchments; and the librarian, who was a man of information, told me that two heaps of papers like these, mouldered by time, had already been committed to the flames. What was my surprise to find amid this heap of papers a considerable number of leaves of a copy of the Old Testament in Greek which seemed to me to be one of the most ancient that I had ever seen. The authorities of the monastery allowed me to possess myself of a third of these parchments, or about forty-three leaves, all the more readily as they were designated for the fire. But I could not get them to yield up possession of the remainder. The too lively satisfaction which I had displayed had aroused their suspicions as to the value of the manuscript. I . . . enjoined the monks to take religious care of all such remains which might fall their way.

They allowed him to list the contents of the other eighty-six leaves, and he also copied a few pages of them.

Although this account appears straightforward, it needs to be scrutinised rather carefully. One does not need to be a devout follower of Edward Saïd to recognise in this text the influence of the genre of the narrative of travel in the Orient: the remoteness of the spot, the antiquity of the surroundings, the ignorance of the inhabitants, the high status of the visitor. So well established was the genre, that Alexandre Dumas Père was able to write an account of his visit to the Orient and St Catherine's without having to give himself the trouble of leaving Paris!

See Plate 14

Beyond this general observation, there are a number of ways in which Tischendorf may have been confused. In the first place, it was the custom for baskets to be used in the monastery library for storing books. In fact, some of them may still be seen in the library today (and parts of baskets were found along with the New Finds). One could imagine that Tischendorf confused library baskets with fuel baskets – after all, a basket is a basket – and jumped to the wrong conclusion. Moreover, parchment is very difficult to burn and produces more smell than heat.

The last basket to be used in the library was emptied onto the shelves in 1895.

Again, one wonders how well he was able to communicate with the monk he was talking to; he might have misunderstood what was being said. Did he communicate directly, or was there an interpreter? If so, who? (The dragoman's role will have been to translate between Arabic and German.) It seems that where direct communication was possible, the preferred medium was French, with Greek as a poor alternative. Tischendorf's limitations in speaking (as opposed to reading) Greek are borne out by a story which he tells against himself: during the 1844 visit, he was given an interview with the Patriarch of Alexandria. The patriarch decided to test his visitor's linguistic skills by asking him to read aloud from a printed book. So bizarre was Tischendorf's Leipzig pronunciation that his host pronounced him to be virtually illiterate: 'How could I read a manuscript, when I could not even read a printed text?' Was Tischendorf able effectively to communicate with the monks? Even granting that he could, one might even suppose another possibility: that the monk had a sense of humour, or else was interested to see how strongly this western visitor would react to such a piece of information.

In short, although there are no grounds for believing it to be deliberately misleading, one cannot take Tischendorf's account at face value. We can suppose that, even with the best will in the world, he may have wanted to believe that he had a role to play in saving the manuscript for posterity. His account asks us to believe a remarkable thing, namely that having looked after this precious manuscript for centuries, the monks were finally destroying it just at the moment – happy coincidence – when a saviour arrived out of the West. Of course, truth is stranger than fiction. But we have seen (in the last chapter) evidence which suggests that parts of the Codex had already been dismembered. We may now add to this the evidence from what Tischendorf saw.

In 1844, he was shown two blocks of material, namely Quires 35-1 to 37-3 and 47-49. He was not shown the leaves in between them, nor anything after. In 1859, he saw Quires 37-4 to 46-8 and 57 onwards. We can say that the material he saw in 1844 was not bound in with what he saw later. It is interesting that the leaf Q34-F8 was not among the 1844 leaves, but among what was shown him in 1859. It adds to the evidence that leaves of the manuscript were kept in different places in the monastery.

WESTERN VISITORS TO SINAI

The fact that the books of the library were of importance to the community is understood when we set Tischendorf's account alongside those of other visitors to Sinai. Indeed, he was one in a long line of those who clung to camels all the way from Cairo. One of the most famous was William John Bankes, collector of Egyptian antiquities which still grace the family seat at Kingston Lacy, Dorset. His visit in August 1815 is described by his companion William Turner. Turner had just been to the monastery, where he was told that they only had three Bibles. 'But Mr Bankes by persevering and rummaging, found out a library of 2,000 volumes, of which three-quarters were MSS, and of these, nine-tenths were Greek.' Turner reports that Bankes 'brought away' five of these books. It is not clear whether this means that he bought, was given, or simply took them. Be that as it may, one of them is still at Kingston Lacy. The other four are back at St Catherine's.

In 1839, Henry Tattam, Coptologist and Archdeacon of Bedford, and his stepdaughter Eliza Platt paid a visit. According to the latter's memoir, Tattam asked to collate 'the valuable Greek MS. of the Gospels which is preserved here'. The monk with whom he had dealings

had from day to day evaded his request to be permitted to see it, until this last day, when he took him into the Archbishop's Room, where it is now kept; and, placing the MS. in his hands, informed him that he had no objection himself to show it to travellers; but that an Englishman, visiting the Convent some time since, had offered the sum of *300l.* for it; upon which he immediately wrote to the Greek Bishop in Cairo respecting the proposal, and, in reply, received orders, 'as it was so valuable, not to part with it on any account whatever'.

Among other things, this account shows that even if St Catherine's was not prey to the coachloads of tourists that now descend upon it daily, there was no shortage of foreign visitors. Interesting also that this is another opportunity which finally arose as the visitor was about to depart.

We can say, then, that Tischendorf's account has been taken at face value by western scholarship for too long, and that there are serious difficulties with it. Parchment will not burn. Even if it did, the burning of Codex Sinaiticus is disproved by the discovery of fragments used in bookbinding and above all by the New Finds of 1975! Finally, it is important to recognise that no other record of the events of 1844 has yet been identified, so that his report lacks corroboration.

THE LEIPZIG LEAVES

What happened next was the acquisition of the forty-three leaves which Tischendorf had been given. He took them back with him to Leipzig and deposited them in the University Library, giving them the name Codex Friderico-Augustanus, in acknowledgement of his patron the King of Saxony, Frederick Augustus II. Tischendorf published a transcription in lithographic facsimile of these leaves in 1846. To understand the significance of this find, we have to remember certain things. First, that this was a part of the Septuagint, and there was no way then of more than hoping that there might be more. But a fourth-century copy of part of the Septuagint is no trivial discovery. It upstaged Codex Ephraemi Rescriptus. Codex Vaticanus, a competitor in terms of age, was still only incompletely known. And the leaves of 1844 are some of the most remarkable in the Codex, containing as they do the extensive Pamphilian corrections to 2 Esdras and Esther with their accompanying colophons, and the three crosses note. One may understand Tischendorf's enthusiasm for the Codex, and the sense of urgency which led him first to seek to buy more through an intermediary, and then to return to St Catherine's to search again. It is worth adding that he refused to reveal where he had found the manuscript. In a letter to his brother written on 15 June shortly after he got back to Cairo, he mentions the manuscript but without referring to the circumstances by which he came to see it. The published account did not come out until 1865. This is hardly surprising, given his hope of finding more. It is not even that one might suspect him of wanting to keep the glory for himself. The acquisition of such things would probably have appeared to an observer then, as now, to be a delicate process in which the intervention of more parties might well have complicated matters. I do not even mean that such an intervention might affect the price. It simply makes the transaction more difficult.

But one aspect of this part of the story may be surprising, namely the fact of ancient manuscripts changing hands. It should be remembered that books are among the more portable of artefacts, as

This was before Bismarck and the unification of Germany. In those days Leipzig was one of the main cities of the Kingdom of Saxony, whose capital was Dresden.

the title of the first chapter of this book reminds us. It had been common since the Renaissance for western Europeans to acquire books from eastern libraries, and interest was increasing in the early part of the nineteenth century. The tone may be set with a quotation from the Honourable Robert Curzon's popular accounts of his bibliophilic travels in the East in the 1830s, *Visits to Monasteries in the Levant*, published in 1849. His visit thus pre-dated Tischendorf's, and his book post-dated it. In the preface to a printing of 1869, Curzon commented on 'the great difference in the habits and manners of the same countries which has taken place within the last thirty years'.

Curzon may have been the source of information for the reference to Codex Sinaiticus in the letter to George Borrow, quoted in the previous chapter.

The most successful miner among the hidden stores of ancient lore has been Mr. Tischendorf, who not only dug out the famous *Codex Sinaiticus* from the convent of St Catherine, but he has rescued from destruction and brought to civilised Europe fifty uncial manuscripts, perfect and imperfect. Some of these I must have seen many years ago, but the monks refused to sell them to me; now they have become more wise. . . . In my transactions I always asked the superior of the monastery whether he was inclined to part with any of his useless books. If he consented to do so, well and good, but if he did not I dropped the question . . .

'Uncial' means the same as majuscule.

In other words, Curzon sought manuscripts but did not importune his hosts. His most dramatic account is of his visit to the Souriani Monastery at the Natron Lakes in Egypt where he found a 'small closet vaulted with stone which was filled to the depth of two feet or more with the loose leaves of the Syriac manuscripts which now form one of the chief treasures of the British Museum' (p. 110).

At the monastery of Balaam at Meteora, on the other hand, Curzon was unable to buy anything:

it was of no use to the monks themselves, who cannot read either Hellenic or ancient Greek; but they consider the books in their library as sacred relics and preserve them with a certain feeling of awe for their antiquity and incomprehensibility. Our only chance is when some world minded agoumenos happens to be at the head of the community, who may be inclined to exchange some of the unreadable old books for such a sum of gold or silver as will suffice for the repairs of one of their buildings, the replenishing of the cellar, or some other equally important purpose. (p. 245)

Various adjectives may be applied to this account, such as cynical and patronising. At the same time it encapsulates the entire relationship when it came to dealings between European adventurers and Orthodox communities. The visitors assume that both their culture and their faith is of a superior brand, and that manuscripts will be safer in their collections than where they are; the hosts respond to this in a variety of ways, including respect for their tradition and balancing the advantages of books over cash for necessary or desirable projects.

On the one hand, western purchases may well have ensured the safety of precious documents, and certainly stimulated the study of Christian antiquity. On the other hand, there might have been other safe places to deposit manuscripts. We should remember that Curzon bought from Mount Athos, a principal store of Byzantine treasures, so it was not only little-known monasteries on the outskirts of the old Byzantine world that were prepared to sell their manuscripts. Indeed most of the larger research libraries contain at least one manuscript which came there from Athos.

In this setting, the purchase by a German scholar of some leaves of a dismembered ancient Septuagint was not out of the ordinary, and we would be wrong to blame either Tischendorf or the monastery for the roles they played. Leipzig University Library is not the only library holding manuscripts from St Catherine's, and Codex Sinaiticus is not the only manuscript from St Catherine's in a western library.

But not everyone was in favour of the sale of manuscripts to western visitors. Later, in 1858, the Holy Synod in St Petersburg was to propose that instead of funding Tischendorf to collect manuscripts, a few young Russian scholars should be sent to take photographs of any significant manuscripts they should find. Certainly the advent of the camera was to change the situation completely. But this option was not available in 1844.

THE VISIT OF 1859

This then, a typical event in its day, was the first dealing between Tischendorf and St Catherine's. The second, in 1853, proved an anticlimax so far as Codex Sinaiticus was concerned. All that Tischendorf found was a little fragment containing eleven lines from Genesis in a collection of lives of saints. According to his son-in-law's account, it was in use as a bookmark. There was no sign of anything else, and the librarian had no recollection of what had happened to the leaves which Tischendorf had seen in 1844. The visitor went home with other treasures, but no further forward in this respect. When he returned in 1859, things got exciting again. This time, Tischendorf had imperial patronage. We resume his account:

Several motives, and more especially the deep reverence of all Eastern monasteries for the Emperor of Russia, led me, in the autumn of 1856, to submit to the Russian Government a plan of a journey for making systematic researches in the East. . . The interest which my proposal excited, even within the imperial circle, inclined the Emperor in my favour. It obtained his approval in the month of September, 1858 . . . and in the commencement of January, 1859, I again set sail for the East . . .

After having devoted a few days in turning over the manuscripts of the convent . . . I told my Bedouins, on the 4th February, to hold themselves in readiness to set out with their dromedaries for Cairo on the 7th, when an entirely fortuitous circumstance carried me at once to the goal of all my desires. On the afternoon of this day I was taking a walk with the steward of the convent in the neighbourhood, and as we returned towards sunset he begged me to take some refreshment with him in his cell. Scarcely had he entered the room, when, resuming our former subject of conversation, he said 'And I too, have read a Septuagint;' and so saying, he took down from the corner of the room a bulky kind of volume wrapped up in a red cloth, and laid it before me. I unrolled the cover, and discovered, to my great surprise, not only those fragments which, fifteen years before, I had taken out of the basket, but also other parts of the Old Testament, the New Testament complete, and, in addition, the Epistle of Barnabas and a part of the Pastor of Hermas.

Again Tischendorf's version requires scrutiny. Fortunately, we are now able to form a far fuller picture of the events which followed and their complicated background.

In order to understand what follows, it is necessary to know the extent and sources of the documentary evidence now available. First, there are papers in Russia which have been the subject of several studies. Second, there is previously unstudied material in St Catherine's. This consists partly of correspondence and other papers which have been there since the events in question. There is also a set of papers which were copied in June 1940. There was at that time still a White Russian embassy in Cairo, and the monastery had copies made of the documents held there which related to Codex Sinaiticus. We are no longer dependent upon later reports by Tischendorf and others.

Moreover, we have available a new document which allows the history of Codex Sinaiticus to be studied from a fresh perspective. This is the agreed account between the four partners in the Codex Sinaiticus Project. It is a text which, in its own words, recognizes that the events are not fully known: 'hence, they are susceptible to widely divergent interpretations and recountings that are evaluated differently as to their form and essence. Although they have not come to a full accord over the recent history of the Codex, the four collaborating institutions offer the present, common, agreed text as the basis of a common formulation, as a framework of historical reference that may be completed by yet further documents, and as a basis for dialogue and the interpretation of events'. The following account draws on the full range of documentation, viewing it in the light of this courageous and far-sighted achievement.

The full text of the account may be read on the project website at http://www.codex sinaiticus.org/en/ codex/history.aspx

COPYING THE MANUSCRIPT

In the first place, Tischendorf wanted to transcribe the manuscript. Affairs at this point were confused by the fact that a new archbishop was to be elected. The Prior, the only person with the authority to allow him to borrow it for this purpose, had left for Cairo. Tischendorf received permission for the loan and sent off a Bedouin, who returned in nine days with the manuscript. Once the manuscript was in Cairo, Tischendorf was able to borrow a quire at a time to make the transcription.

Meanwhile, the process of installing a new archbishop was not proving straightforward. The nominee was Cyril, to be the second archbishop of that name. The consecration had to be carried out by the Patriarch of Jerusalem, who was opposed to Cyril's appointment. The difficulties arising out of this situation had both an immediate and a more lasting influence. To start with, they complicated the process of making a transcription of the manuscript. They were also an important factor in the chain of events which led to the presentation of the manuscript to the Tsar. They have also been responsible for some of the subsequent misunderstandings and controversy surrounding this presentation.

It needs to be stated again that Tischendorf's goal was to produce printed editions of ancient manuscripts, so as to preserve their contents for posterity. The edition of Codex Sinaiticus was a continuation of the project he had set himself at the beginning of his career:

In the first place my object is to collect the few manuscripts of the text of the New Testament written before the tenth century and lying dispersed through the libraries of Europe, and print them verbatim. This collection of originals, which would comprise thirty to forty volumes, appears to me on one side to present a far safer foundation for the learned critics of the text of all ages than the comparison of lists of various readings; and on the other side I consider it in itself a valuable possession for the Christian church.

The most important task for him was therefore to record the contents. This he set out to do at once in Cairo:

The time was now come boldly and without delay to set to work to a task of transcribing no less than a hundred and ten thousand lines, – of which a great number were difficult to read, either on account of later corrections, or through the ink having faded, – and that in a climate where the thermometer during March, April, and May, is never below 77° in the shade. No one can say what this cost me in fatigue and exhaustion.

According to his son-in-law, Tischendorf accomplished the task in two months, with the assistance of two Germans resident in Cairo, a doctor and a chemist (in some accounts they are an apothecary and a bookseller). Their role was to copy out the manuscript, and Tischendorf checked their work. No doubt they achieved a great deal. But why does Tischendorf's own account go on to state that when in September he took the manuscript as a loan to St Petersburg, it was 'there to have it copied as accurately as possible'? And that it was to take a further three years to complete 'the laborious task of producing a *facsimile* copy of this codex in four folio volumes'? Is it true that in those two months in Cairo they transcribed the whole manuscript? Or at any rate, that what they produced was more than the rough beginnings of a transcription? The experience of the Digital Project (building on a hundred and fifty years of research) suggests that eight weeks might serve to produce some sort of a version of some of the manuscript, but not an accurate copy of the whole.

But it is the outcome that matters, and the facsimile edition is a wonderful achievement, transferring the manuscript into book form, with layout and font intended to represent those of the See Plate 15 manuscript, and with detailed notes describing the corrections. Tischendorf not only had to make a transcription, he had to ascertain the number of scribes, allocate the text to each, and do the same for all the correctors. Areas where he was at fault have already been mentioned. But on the whole he laid safe foundations for subsequent research. The triumphant denouement came when

In the month of October, 1862, I repaired to St. Petersburg to present this edition to their Majesties. The Emperor, who had liberally provided the cost, and who approved the proposal of this superb manuscript appearing on the celebration of the Millenary Jubilee of the Russian empire, has distributed impressions of it throughout the Christian world, which, without distinction of creed, have expressed their recognition of its value.

PRESENTATION TO THE TSAR

St Catherine's Monastery had received support and gifts from Russia since the fourteenth century. The bonds were strong, and the appearance in Sinai of a German academic may have been a far less significant part of the story than has often been supposed. Tischendorf indeed brought Codex Sinaiticus to the attention of many people; but the relationship between the monastery and the imperial court was a much more important matter to the community than its dealings with western travellers.

We may put the matter into context by telling the story of Tischendorf's Russian equivalent, Archimandrite Porphyry Uspenski (also baptised Constantin). Uspenski visited St Catherine's shortly after Tischendorf's first visit. He saw the manuscript, and it appears that Tischendorf's success in becoming the one whose name was most closely associated with it came to rankle him. In 1863 he published a bad-tempered attack on the manuscript, observing that 'the people looked affectionately on the relic of Sinaitic antiquity, and kissed it devoutly, knowing nothing of its heretical origin, neither perceiving any foul odour from it'. (The supposed heresy is due to the text's differences from the Byzantine text of later centuries.) Although this attack has the odour of sour grapes about it, it did not need Tischendorf's equally ill-tempered rejoinder against the 'dirty controversy of a stupid and fanatical monk, who is full of absurd petty jealousy'. But this is only one part of the relationship between the two men. In 1862 Uspenski was extremely generous in sharing his finds with Tischendorf, who wrote warmly of his generosity and their cordial dealings.

The manuscript had been made temporarily available in Cairo. To move it to St Petersburg was more convenient for Tischendorf to continue making his transcription. It must be remembered that he was on this trip under the imperial patronage. Taking his discoveries to St Petersburg will have been the natural result of such an expedition. So the next event was the completion of a loan of the manuscript, made in the autumn. This document, signed by Tischendorf and dated in September 1859, has given rise to the belief that it was borrowed and never returned, that Tischendorf defaulted on his promise; to be blunt, that the manuscript was stolen. But it is not the only relevant document.

Was any more permanent arrangement agreed in 1859? According to Tischendorf, it was he who first suggested to the monks that they present the manuscript to the Tsar. Whether the idea was his alone may be considered more doubtful. We have partial corroboration in a letter from Prince Lobanov to the Sinai community dated 10/22 September, stating that 'Mr. Tischendorf informed me that the honourable brotherhood of Mt. Sinai has undertaken to bring to His Majesty the Emperor Alexander II through his mediation an old Bible manuscript'. The letter observed that this could not be effected until the new archbishop had been recognised by the Sublime Porte and that the manuscript remained the property of the monastery: 'It is obvious that if unforeseen circumstances prevent the Brotherhood from concluding this intention, the manuscript will be returned without any hesitation'. In its Act No. 6 of 16 September, the Sinai brotherhood responded to this letter by agreeing that the manuscript should be entrusted, as a loan, to Tischendorf, 'and in accordance with the terms contained in the letter'. In a letter to Lobanov on 29 September, the community expressed itself in similarly broad terms. The Russian view of the situation is found in

Two dates are given because Russia and St Catherine's were still using the Julian Calendar, which was then twelve days behind the Gregorian.

a letter from Lobanov to the Foreign Ministry on 5/17 April 1860: 'The desire of the brethren of Sinai to present the manuscript to His Majesty the Emperor was communicated to me by Cyril Archbishop of Sinai before his ordination in Constantinople; in doing so, the Sinai community meant both to oblige His Majesty the Emperor, who sent Mr. Tischendorf to Sinai to find old copies of the Scriptures, and to obtain our Embassy's support for the appointment of their Archbishop.' We can say therefore that the idea of a donation was raised, but not that the evidence shows it to have been universally approved.

For the next three years, Tischendorf examined the manuscript in St Petersburg regularly while making the edition. On 29 October 1862, he passed it over to the Russian authorities, at the point at which he presented his edition to the Tsar and Tsarina. The manuscript, which remained the possession of the monastery, was placed in the Ministry for Foreign Affairs in St Petersburg. The question arose as to whether it should be returned to the monastery pending resolution of the donation question, but the monastery does not appear to have made a clear request, and the idea was left in abeyance while affairs relating to the archbishopric of Sinai were sorted out. It is to this that we now turn, going back to the year 1859.

We resume the story with the reluctance of the Patriarch of Jerusalem (and subsequent events suggest that his reservations were worth taking seriously) to consecrate Cyril.

Archbishop Cyril

The Synaxis ('assembly') is here the governing body composed of all the members of the community (it can also mean something like the executive body of the monastery).

In due course, Cyril's appointment was properly ratified by both the ecclesiastical and the Ottoman authorities. But it did not turn out happily. His relationship with the rest of the community steadily deteriorated until the point in 1865 when some of the monks were physically attacked by Cyril's servants and then exiled from the monastery. In August 1866, the Synaxis deposed Cyril and elected Kallistratos in his place. It was to take three years for the new archbishop to be recognised by all the necessary ecclesiastical and civil authorities. Meanwhile, the Russian government sequestrated the monastery's income from lands in their territories. Throughout this period, Cyril was in Constantinople and trying to maintain his position.

The breakdown in the relationship between the archbishop and the monastery led to a paralysis in the discussions as to what was to be done with Codex Sinaiticus. Between 1862 and 1868, Tischendorf wrote regularly to Cyril to press the matter, without receiving any very clear answer.

The donation

Shortly after Kallistratos had been recognised by the ecumenical patriarch, Tischendorf went to St Petersburg to try yet again to push matters on. The Tsar instructed that Count Ignatiev take over as intermediary, and that Tischendorf's role in the negotiations should be brought to an end.

Count Ignatiev, Ambassador to the Grand Porte, was in an ideal situation to carry on the transactions, and in May of 1868 he contacted both the old and the new archbishop to ascertain the community's mind on the matter. Not surprisingly, he received contradictory replies. The deposed Cyril claimed that the community had never had any intention of donating the manuscript. On 5 July, Archbishop Kallistratos informed Ignatiev directly that the community considered the manuscript to have been given to the Tsar from the day it was passed to Tischendorf. The Cairo Synaxis of St Catherine's had (on 28 June) written to the Russian vice consul in Egypt a letter which reached Ignatiev a few days later:

With utter affliction the Holy Synaxis of fathers and all the brethren of Sinai recently have learnt that our ex-Archbishop Cyril, that terrible wrecker of our holy and glorious Monastery, alleges that the Sinai community unanimously rose against him and banished him because he had offered the ancient manuscript of the Gospels to the Emperor of all Russia and protector of Orthodoxy, and that allegedly we intend to claim

143

back the aforementioned manuscript, using the affidavit of the Imperial Embassy in Constantinople, which was then headed by Prince Lobanov. Therefore we consider it our sacred duty to make it clear to your Serenity, and through your Serenity to the Imperial Embassy and all the higher authorities, that all these rumours are nothing other than the inventions of a slanderer, who thought that by distorting the truth he could harm our miserable Monastery, which has already suffered so much from him. So we state our case.

A few years ago Constantin Tischendorf arrived at Sinai with a letter of recommendation to the fathers from Prince Lobanov, who was then Ambassador, in which the latter asked us to cede the aforementioned ancient manuscript of the New Testament for copying, and guaranteed that after copying the manuscript would be returned. Having considered the letter of recommendation, we lent it for copying. We then thought that besides this manuscript Sinai has nothing more precious to offer to the Greatest Emperor, the protector of Orthodoxy and of ourselves and wished to express our endless gratitude and devotion to His divinely guarded Majesty . . . We are sure that the deception will be easily comprehended and that His Excellency General Ignatiev will be completely convinced in our right and in the right of the Monastery, and will order, as it befits the glorious representative of Holy Russia, that the money withheld under the ex-Archbishop of Holy Sinai would be paid to us, and that he will promote the quicker arrival here of the reverend Archbishop Kallistratos, our legitimate and true pastor.

The letter was accompanied by Prince Lobanov's letter of 10 September 1859, and Act 6 of 16 September 1859. The 'money withheld' refers to the income which the Russian authorities had sequestrated, and which the community sorely needed. The 'quicker arrival of the archbishop' may refer to the fact that on Russian prompting the Viceregent of Egypt had yet to give him permission to enter Egypt.

At the same time, two letters from Count Ignatiev to Archimandrite Antonin Kapustin of the Russian Mission in Jerusalem reveal that the Synaxis' letter should be read in the light of its final sentence. In the first letter, of May 8/20 1868, he writes

Could you not arrange for us another small matter . . . ? In other words, could you help me put an end to the [story that the Sinai Bible was stolen by us]? . . . It is necessary to obtain from the Sinai Monastery a document certifying that the precious manuscript was offered as a gift to the Emperor; we could give 3–4 medals instead, of different orders, maybe 10 or 12 thousand roubles over and above, as well; the less the better, and we will be more grateful to you. . . . Maybe with our promise to recognize the new archbishop of Sinai . . . it will be possible to accomplish the case cheaply, just with medals . . .

His second letter, of June 18/30, is even blunter:

As soon as the Bible has been offered as a gift to the Emperor (at less cost to the Government), the hindrances to the solution of all the Sinai difficulties will be lifted . . . De Lex announced here and at Petersburg that the Sinai brotherhood is ready to offer the Bible for free, since in Sinai it is considered a Russian property, provided Kallistratos is recognized and the Monastery is allowed to receive the money sequestrated by us. Such a saving of money (I mean the payment of the manuscript just for our consent to the enthronement of Kallistratos and for the donation of someone else's money) pleased greatly the dignitaries in Petersburg, and especially the Chancellor. . . . What do you think about it? For the time being, I answered that I find it more decent to give a sum, however modest, so that it would be possible to say that we had bought the Bible rather than purloined it.

It is clear enough that the codex was a bargaining tool in the wider business of recognising Kallistratos and releasing the part of the monastery's income that was being held back until the situation had been regularised. In the same tone, Ignatiev wrote on 31 July to Nikolaev, his vice consul in Egypt, that

I consider it necessary confidentially to inform you that the formal declaration of the Sinai brotherhood that the well known manuscript Bible belonging to the Monastery has been donated to His Imperial Majesty the Emperor and is Imperial property has been set as the condition for his [Kallistratos'] recognition.

The words in square brackets are ambiguous. They could also mean the 'episode of the Bible stolen by us'.

145

The final stages would take some time to complete. An official act of donation received by Count Ignatiev in September 1868 was signed only by Archbishop Kallistratos and the members of the Synaxis of Sinai's metochion in Cairo, and in any case Kallistratos had yet to have his position recognised by the Egyptian government. Although Count Ignatiev had already (late in 1868) received from St Petersburg 9,000 roubles and various medals assigned to the archbishop and the community of Sinai for the donation of the Codex, he decided to wait until a properly signed act of donation had been issued. It was not until a visit to Egypt in November 1869, when Ignatiev met Archbishop Kallistratos in Cairo, that he was to receive another act of donation, signed by the archbishop, the members of the Cairo metochion's Synaxis (on 13 November 1869) and the members of St Catherine's Synaxis (on 18 November 1869). On 5 January 1870 the Russian consul in Egypt passed the 9,000 roubles and medals to Archbishop Kallistratos and the members of the Sinai community. This part of Codex Sinaiticus was now Codex Sinaiticus Petropolitanus, and was placed in the Imperial Public Library.

The monastery's official acknowledgement of the roubles and medals expresses thanks for them, but does not refer to them as payment for the Codex.

One strange twist to the tale is that the act of 18 November 1869 does not seem to have been entered in the monastery's official record, and has not been found elsewhere in the monastery's archives.

Now that we have access to all the documents, what are we to make of them?

First, that it is a far more complicated story than has often been recognised. Within it, the role of Tischendorf is important from the scholarly point of view. In terms of the donation of the manuscript, his part was in the end a minor one. The most important issue here is the long and close relationship between St Catherine's and Russia.

Second, it is clear that the Codex was used as a bargaining tool by the Russian authorities. Incidentally, the fact that it was so successful

A metochion is a dependency of a monastery, sometimes acting as an embassy of one autonomous church to another, in this case of St Catherine's to the patriarchate in Cairo.

a tool is yet another indication of the status of Codex Sinaiticus. One may also marvel that its acquisition was so important to the imperial government that it was prepared to go to such lengths.

Third, although this documentation provides only a limited insight into whatever discussions were held by the community of St Catherine's, we may surmise that they may have felt that they had very little choice once the manuscript had been away for ten years, and when its return was balanced against the confirmation of their new archbishop in his office and the restoration of their full revenues.

Traditionally, interpretations of the story have centred around Tischendorf, treating him either as hero or as villain. The extensive research conducted within the Codex Sinaiticus Project, including thorough discussions among the Project partners, has revealed something far more complex, one indeed in which we are encouraged to understand how the protagonists were limited either by circumstance or by the current ethos rather than to judge them. We now have a much greater shared understanding of the events of a century and a half ago, and a firm foundation for continued discussion. As Codex Sinaiticus has been virtually reunited across its four locations, so the Project has brought us closer in our understanding of its history.

SOURCES AND FURTHER READING

The account by Tischendorf is published in *When were our Gospels Written? An Argument by Constantine Tischendorf. With a Narrative of the Discovery of the Sinaitic Manuscript*, London: Religious Tract Society, 1866 (quotations from a new edition, 1890, with slight changes). The original account, *Wann wurden unsere Evangelien verfasst?*, Leipzig: J. C. Hinrichs'sche Verlag, 1865, 'attracted' (in the words of the translator) 'great attention on its first publication; but as it was written in the technical style in which German professors are accustomed to address their students and the learned classes generally, it was felt that a revision of this pamphlet, in a more popular form and adapted to general readers, would meet a want of the age' (p. 3). For information about the different editions, and translations into a number of modern languages, see C. Böttrich, *Bibliographie Konstantin von Tischendorf (1815–1874)*, Leipzig: Leipziger Universitätsverlag, 1999, pp. 37–39. Note that even the fourth edition of the German appeared in 1866, so that they all pre-date the events of 1869.

The book by Tischendorf's son-in-law is L. Schneller, *Search on Sinai. The Story of Tischendorf's Life and the Search for a Lost Manuscript*, London: Epworth Press, 1939.

For other travellers to Sinai, see references in many wider accounts. The book by Dumas is discussed by M. Taymanova, 'Alexandre Dumas in Egypt: Mystification or Truth?', in P. Starkey and J. Starkey (eds), *Travellers in Egypt*, London and New York: I. B. Tauris, 1998, pp. 181–88. There is an account of Bankes in P. Usick, *Adventures in Egypt and Nubia. The Travels of William John Bankes (1786–1855)*, London: British Museum Press, 2002. Curzon's *Visits to Monasteries in the Levant* is quoted from an edition with an introduction by Seton Dearden and preface by Basil Blackwell (Ithaca, N.Y.: Cornell University Press, 1955).

Archdeacon Tattam's travels are recorded by his stepdaughter, Eliza Platt, in *Journal of a Tour through Egypt, the Peninsula of Sinai, and the Holy Land, in 1838, 1839*, 2 vols, privately printed, London, 1841. The first volume is available through Google Book Search. The visit to St Catherine's is recorded in the second.

The extensive researches on the Donation include the paper by Dr Anna Zakharova, which may be viewed at http://www.nlr.ru/eng/exib/CodexSinaiticus/zah/3.html. Professor Christfried Böttrich's account will be published separately. The translation of the Cairo Synaxis' letter of 28 June 1868 is Dr Zakharova's, and those of the letters of Count Ignatiev are by Dr Fyssas, with a few re-phrasings. Note that Dr Zakharova's translation of the Synaxis' letter at http://www.nlr.ru/eng/exib/CodexSinaiticus/zah/3_5.html differs slightly from the version above in its interpretation of the penultimate clause.

The quotation concerning Tischendorf's goals in his research is taken from pp. 6–7 of M. Black and R. Davidson, *Constantin von Tischendorf and the Greek New Testament*, Glasgow: University of Glasgow Press, 1981.

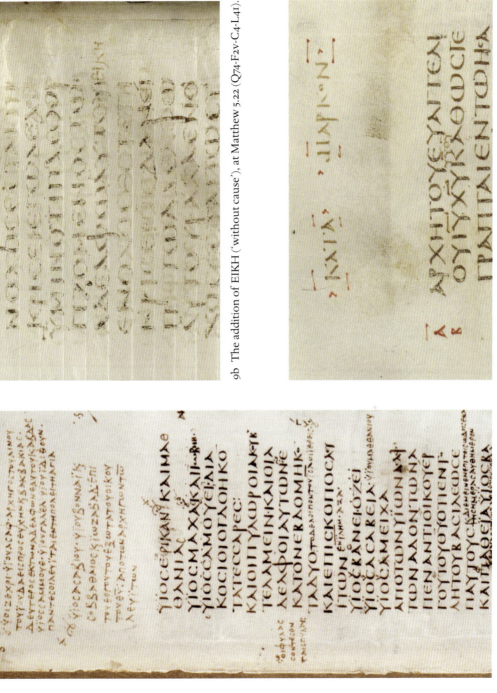

9a Q36-F4r-C1, showing the Pamphilian Corrector's additions to the text of 2 Esdras.

9b The addition of EIKH ('without cause'), at Matthew 5.22 (Q74-F2v-C4-L41).

9c Q76-F2-C1, the first page of Mark's Gospel, with the correction 'Son of God' added above the line in line 2.

ΜΑΓΩΥΓΕ	ΔΙΚΝΥΜΙΕΑΝΤΑ	ΕΛΛΟΥΝΓ
ΝΩΠΕΡΙ	ΓΛΩΣΣΑΙΣΤΩΝΑ	ΟΣΕΦΡΟΝ
ΟΥΣΤΙΜΗ	ΘΡΩΠΩΝΛΑΛΩΚ	ΝΗΠΙΟΣΕ
ΙΗΣΧΙΣΜΑ	ΤΩΝΑΓΓΕΛΩΝΑΓΑ	ΜΗΝΩΣΝ
ΟΣΩΜΑΤΙ	ΠΗΝΔΕΜΗΕΧΩ	ΟΤΕΓΕΓΟΝΑ
ΑΥΤΟΥΠΕ	ΟΥΘΕΝΕΙΜΙ	ΚΑΤΗΡΓΗΚ
ΧΩΝΜΕΡΙ	ΚΑΙΕΑΝΨΩΜΙΣΩ	ΝΗΠΙΟΥ
ΓΑΜΕΛΗ	ΠΑΝΤΑΤΑΥΠΑΡΧ	ΒΛΕΠΟΜΕΝ
ΕΠΑΣΧΕΙΝ	ΤΑΜΟΥΚΑΙΕΑΝΠΑ	ΤΙΔΙΕΣΟΠΤ
ΟΥΝΠΑΣΧΕΙ	ΡΑΔΩΤΟΣΩΜΑΜ	ΝΑΙΝΙΓΜΑ
ΤΑΜΕΛΗ	ΙΝΑΚΑΥΧΗΣΩΜΑ	ΔΕΠΡΟΣΩ
ΣΑΖΕΤΑΙΜ	ΑΓΑΠΗΝΔΕΜΗΕ	ΠΡΟΣΩΠΟ
ΧΑΙΡΕΙΤΑ	ΧΩΟΥΘΕΝΩΦ	ΓΙΝΩΣΚΩ
ΕΛΗ	ΜΑΙ	ΡΟΥΣΤΟΔΕ
ΕΕΣΤΕΣΩ	ΗΑΓΑΠΗ	ΣΟΜΑΙΚΛΟ
ΑΙΜΕΛΗΚ	ΜΑΚΡΟΘΥΜΕΙ	ΕΠΕΓΝΩΣ
ΣΚΑΙΟΥΣΜ	ΧΡΗΣΤΕΥΕΤΑΙ	ΝΥΝΙΔΕΜΕ
ΟΟΣΕΝΤΗΚ	ΗΑΓΑΠΗ	ΠΙΣΤΙΣΕΛΠ
ΑΙΠΡΩΤΟΝ	ΟΥΖΗΛΟΙ	ΤΑΤΡΙΑΤΑΥΤ
ΟΛΟΥΣ	ΗΑΓΑΠΗ	ΔΕΤΟΥΤΩΝ
ΟΝ	ΟΥΠΕΡΠΕΡΕΥΕΤΑ	ΠΗΔΙΩΚΕΤ
ΙΤΑΣ	ΟΥΦΥΣΙΟΥΤΑΙ	ΑΓΑΠΗΝ
	ΟΥΚΑΣΧΗΜΟΝΕΙ	ΖΗΛΟΥΤΕΛΕΤ
ΑΛΟΥΣ	ΟΥΖΗΤΕΙΤΑΕΑΥΤΗΣ	ΚΑΙΜΑΛΛΟΝ
ΔΥΝΑΜΙΣ	ΟΥΠΑΡΟΞΥΝΕΤΑΙ	ΝΑΠΡΟΦΗ
ΧΑΡΙΣΜΑ	ΟΥΛΟΓΙΖΕΤΑΙΤΟΚΑ	ΤΕΟΓΑΡΛΑΛ
ΤΩΝ	ΟΥΧΑΙΡΕΙΕΠΙΤΗΑ	ΓΛΩΣΣΗΟΥ
ΙΜΤΕΙΣ	ΔΙΚΙΑΣΥΓΧΑΙΡΙ	ΘΡΩΠΟΙΣ
ΗΙΣΙΤΑΩ	ΤΗΑΛΗΘΙΑ	ΑΛΛΑΘΩΟΥ
	ΠΑΝΤΑΣΤΕΓΕΙ	ΑΚΟΥΕΙΠΝΙ
ΕΣ	ΠΑΝΤΑΠΙΣΤΕΥΕΙ	ΔΕΙΜΥΣΤΗ
ΟΛΟΙ	ΠΑΝΤΑΕΛΠΙΖΕΙ	ΔΕΠΡΟΦΗ
ΤΕΣ	ΠΑΝΤΑΥΠΟΜΕΝΕΙ	

10 1 Corinthians 13 (Q83-F4r-C3): in the upper margin is the supplied text for the omission at verses 2–3 (with a running title to the left of it). The sequence of short lines begins at line 14.

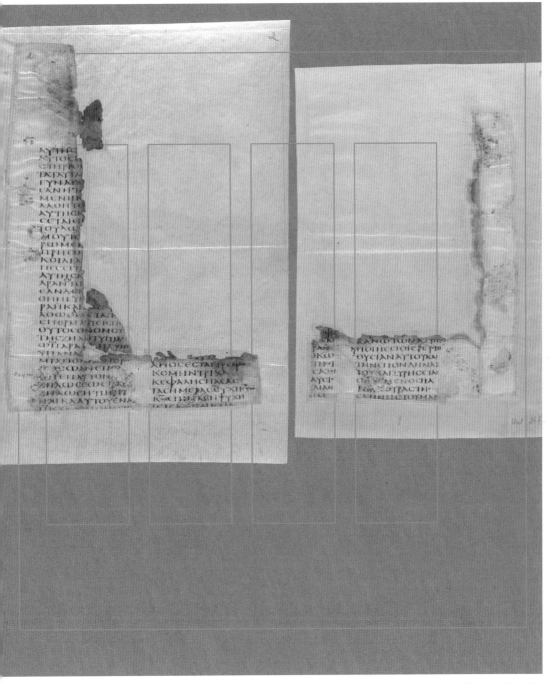

11 Two pieces from the side and bottom margins of Q11-F2, cut up for bookbinding. The recto is illustrated, with the fragments positioned in relation to each other as they were in the full page. The fragments are in the National Library of Russia.

National Library of Russia

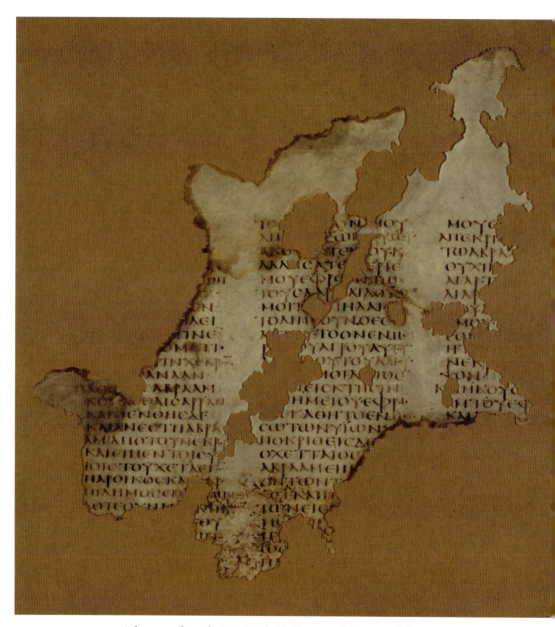

12 A fragment from the New Finds (Q3-F3v, containing part of Genesis 23).

Constantin Tischendorf.

Nach einer Daguerrotype von Bertha Wehnert geb. Beckmann.

13 Tischendorf as a young man in the early 1840s, the period in which he first encountered Codex Sinaiticus. Kupferstich-Kabinett, Staatliche Kunstsammlungen Dresden. Photo: Herbert Boswank

16 Delivery of Codex Sinaiticus to the British Museum on 27 December 1933. Ernest Maggs (*left*) hands the
manuscript to Sir George Hill (*right*). Sir Frederic Kenyon stands between them.
British Library Add Ms 68923, f.1

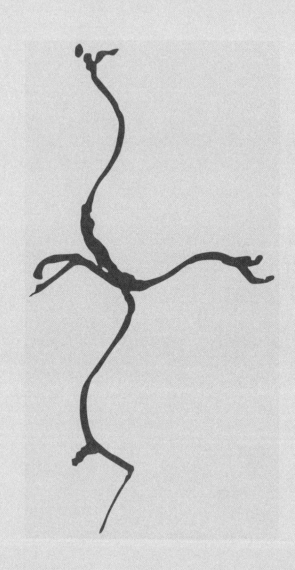

CHAPTER TEN

Beyond the Monastery

THE next episode in the story is of a very different kind. It is a scene from comedy.

SIMONIDES

It is usual for forgers to pass off their work as that of another. It is rare for them to claim authorship of a genuine article. But (and one thing this book should have shown is that Codex Sinaiticus is the kind of manuscript that attracts attention) this happened. The *Manchester Guardian* of 3 September 1862 contained a letter from one C. Simonides, in which he carefully set out the way in which he had made a copy of the Greek Scriptures for presentation by his uncle Benedict, librarian of the Monastery Panteleimon on Mount Athos, to Tsar Nicholas I. He explains the details of how he did this, and of how the Patriarch of Constantinople persuaded him to present the manuscript to St Catherine's, and of the archbishop's letter of thanks for the gift (dated 13 August 1841), of how when he saw it in 1852 it was much altered, looking 'older than it should do', concluding that 'the above is a true statement of the origin and history of the famous Codex Sinaiticus, which Professor Tischendorf has foisted on the world as a MS. of the fourth century', finally explaining that the corrections were made by his uncle. One understands why a former Regius Professor of Greek in the University of Oxford has described

Simonides' as 'a name indeed that deserves a whole page in the golden book of chutzpah'.

Some of Simonides' forgeries of Greek manuscripts had been accepted as genuine, and landed him in prison when they were exposed. The absurdity of his claim to have forged something so indisputably the genuine article must be put down to malice. The fact that Tischendorf was one of those who had exposed Simonides (early in 1856) may have had something to do with it. A few, in the British press at any rate, chose to take the matter up. A long-defunct journal called *The Literary Churchman* actually took Simonides' side, while claiming neutrality. In retrospect, it may seem surprising that anybody could have taken any of Simonides' letter seriously. But one has only to look at more recent cases to see that there is never a dearth of people willing to support a ridiculous claim.

CODICES SINAITICI

Even though most of its leaves are now elsewhere, the Monastery of St Catherine has not ceased to play a role in the continuing history of Codex Sinaiticus, and the Codex has continued to play a role in the life of the monastery.

It might have been the case that its loss could have permanently soured relations between western scholars and the community. That it did not is shown by the much happier story of the Sinaitic Syriac palimpsest, discovered by Agnes Lewis in 1892. This manuscript is a fourth-century copy of an even older translation of the Gospels into Syriac. Both Agnes Lewis and her twin sister Margaret Gibson enjoyed warm friendships with the monks, and several successful visits were made to St Catherine's in order to study the manuscript. Other scholars, such as James Rendel Harris (who once referred to Tischendorf as 'the great brigand of Leipzig'), were also generously welcomed at the monastery.

Times were changing in other ways. 1859, the year of Tischendorf's third visit, saw work begin on the Suez Canal, and

1869 saw its completion. By 1897 the overland journey to the monastery took three days instead of seven. Developments in photography allowed distant manuscripts to be brought into the scholar's study. The young Tischendorf of 1844 stood in a tradition of travellers who moved around in the time-honoured ways, by sail, horse, camel and 'shanks' pony'. Steamships and railways made travel quicker and easier, and put an end to the quaintly provincial view that St Catherine's was a distant place.

World politics changed no less, and what happened next to Codex Sinaiticus was to be due again to events in Russia.

THE CODEX UNDER SOVIET RULE

What happened to Codex Sinaiticus after the Russian Revolution? One anonymous writer to *The Times* (on 20 March 1919) feared that 'the Bolshevik leaders in their mad obsession may have left it to any chance that may befall it'. In fact it was still safe in its library, and the Bolshevik leaders had no intention of destroying such a valuable asset.

The issue of ownership was taken up in 1925, when on 27 July, Archbishop Porphyrios III of Sinai made use of an official visit to Moscow by a representative of the Ecumenical Patriarchate in Constantinople to write to the Soviet government asking for the return of the codex ('I hope that the new Russia, inspired by sentiments of justice and fairness, would wish to make good this evil by restoring the codex to the Convent'). There is no trace of any reply.

Was it as the result of some confused echo of a rumour of the Archbishop's letter that the German press of 25 August 1925, reported 'with considerable flourish' (according to next day's *Times*) that a new fragment of Codex Sinaiticus had been discovered in Berlin? The rumour was scotched by the Director of the Manuscript Department of the Prussian State Library, who pointed out that the Codex already contained that portion of text and that the script of this discovery was twice as large and completely different.

Of manuscripts and Five Year Plans

The 1928 Five Year Plan was devised as a means of industrialising the Russian economy and agriculture as quickly as possible. Success required access to capital for the purchase of goods and machinery. In particular, the Soviet government needed sterling in London banks. One way of raising capital was through the sale of art works (all museums and libraries were by now nationalised), and this was to continue to be the policy in the second Five Year Plan, which immediately succeeded the first. But selling art works is a business that needs careful management. Concern that too many sales could depress the market led the bookdealers Maggs and the auctioneers Sotheby's to try to form a company in order to manage affairs carefully and in the best interests of sellers and dealers (but not buyers). The company was never formed, but the links which were established with Soviet authorities proved useful to Maggs, and led to their acting as agent when the Codex Sinaiticus was offered for sale.

The story of its purchase and of the fundraising which made the acquisition possible is the subject of the next chapter.

> In 1933 the Soviet Union imported fifteen tractors from the USA and manufactured 78,289. Two years before it had imported 23,442 and made 38,282.

SOURCES AND FURTHER READING

For Simonides and chutzpah, see Peter Parsons, 'Forging Ahead. Has Simonides Struck Again?', *Times Literary Supplement*, 22 February 2008, and the letter by Haris Kalligas, 19 March 2008. The episode is extensively documented by J. K. Elliott, *Codex Sinaiticus and the Simonides Affair. An Examination of the Nineteenth Century Claim that Codex Sinaiticus was not an Ancient Manuscript* (Αναλεκτα Βλαταδων 33), Thessaloniki: Patriarchal Institute for Patristic Studies, 1982.

For the story of Agnes Lewis and Margaret Gibson, see J. M. Soskice, *The Sisters of Sinai. How Two Lady Adventurers Discovered the Hidden Gospels*, New York, 2009. This book cannot be recommended too highly as a wonderful biography of two remarkable people, as well as an account of scholarly dealings with the east in the later nineteenth century.

For Soviet Russia in 1933 I depend on *Russia Observed* by Allan Monk-house and on D. G. Dalrymple, 'The American Tractor Comes to Soviet Agriculture: The Transfer of a Technology', *Technology and Culture* 5 (1964), pp. 191–214. See most recently A. Odom and W. R. Salmond (eds), *Treasures into Tractors. The Selling of Russia's Cultural Heritage, 1918–1938*, Seattle: University of Washington Press, 2009.

The quotation from Rendel Harris is in a lecture 'Methods of Research in Eastern Libraries' given in 1895 and printed in James Rendel Harris, *New Testament Autographs and Other Essays*, ed. Alessandro Falcetta (New Testament Monographs 7), Sheffield: Sheffield Phoenix Press, 2006, pp. 72–82, p. 77. The entire essay is worth reading in order to redress the balance with Tischendorf's view of eastern monastic libraries.

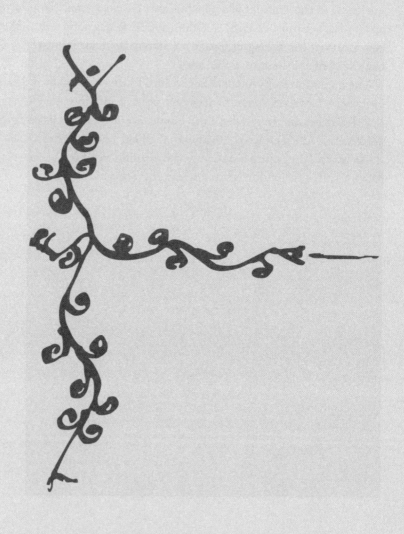

CHAPTER ELEVEN

Codex Sinaiticus Comes to Town

EVERY book its destiny: that was borne out by the story of Codex Sinaiticus in the nineteenth century, when it was selected as the monastery's most precious gift 'to offer to the Greatest Emperor, the protector of Orthodoxy and of ourselves'. Codex Sinaiticus has never been far from the headlines.

THE ACQUISITION

According to a brief history of Maggs produced by the firm, the story begins in 1931. Ernest Maggs and the head of the Paris office, Dr Maurice Ettinghausen, travelled to Leningrad (as Petrograd had been called since 1924). There was so little food that Ettinghausen later claimed to have survived on a diet of canned sardines he had taken with him. But the trip was worth it, because the two men bought a copy of the Gutenberg Bible (pre-sold to Martin Bodmer). They also began the negotiations which were to lead to their purchase of Codex Sinaiticus. The negotiations began with an asking price of £200,000 and an offer of £40,000, before the final price of £100,000 was settled on. This made it by a long way the most expensive book in the world.

British Library research begins in the middle of 1933, when the Soviet government approached Maggs, and Maggs approached a former Director of the British Museum, Sir Frederick Kenyon.

Sir Frederick
Kenyon, known for
books such as *Our
Bible and the Ancient
Manuscripts*. In
those days what is
now the British
Library was a part
of the British
Museum.

Kenyon wasted no time in telling the Board of Trustees. The Chairman was the Archbishop of Canterbury, Cosmo Gordon Lang. Lang at once (7 August) wrote to the Prime Minster, Ramsay MacDonald, asking for the government's support. MacDonald replied two days later that 'I am willing to do everything I possibly can to secure the Codex for the British Museum', and wrote also to the Chancellor of the Exchequer (Neville Chamberlain) advising a government loan to the Museum. Such immediate enthusiasm from MacDonald may seem surprising. The reason lies in the political and economic situation in Britain.

The first Labour prime minister (in 1924), MacDonald led a socialist government from 1929, which in 1931 became a cross-party government (hence the fact that the Chancellor was a Tory). Times were bad and MacDonald was struggling. It seemed a good idea to be seen to support something which might lift the public mood and direct attention elsewhere (the feel-good factor is no new invention). There is also a context in economic theory for the purchase. In March 1933 John Maynard Keynes had published four articles in *The Times* under the title 'The Means to Prosperity', in which he argued that the government should finance public works in order to benefit the economy. The Chancellor was not persuaded, but MacDonald may have seen the purchase of Codex Sinaiticus as a small step in this direction, since it would involve transferring to the Soviet Union funds which would then be invested in buying British resources. At the same time, in the very difficult circumstances of the Depression, spending money to buy a very expensive book from a widely distrusted Soviet government was bound to excite strong emotions, as will come out in the story of the fundraising. Suffice it to say that MacDonald got his way, to the extent that Chamberlain agreed to guarantee a purchase of up to £100,000, so long as the Museum put up £7,000 and launched a public subscription.

There was a delicate game to be played. Chamberlain did not want news of the guarantee to leak, because it might affect the appeal. He favoured a deal which paid after the acquisition of the

158

manuscript. The Museum favoured cash down. So did the Russians. At the same time, there was a view that this was an opportunity not to be missed, someone suggesting that without the Depression the manuscript would have sold for £200,000 in the USA (and in 1936 the University of Texas was to offer the Museum precisely that sum for the Codex, which strangely was the initial Soviet *asking* price). In the end, Sir George Hill (the Director of the British Museum) wrote to the Treasury that the price was agreed, payment to be by cash on delivery. On 18 December, he was able to make a formal offer to Maggs.

£100,000 in 1934 is approximately equivalent to £5 million today. But since appreciation rates for ancient manuscripts have far exceeded the standard rate of inflation, this comparison does not at all reflect the probable value of the manuscript today.

The next task was to transfer the manuscript to London. This was arranged by Arcos, a company trading between the UK and USSR, and in effect a department of the export and import sections of the USSR's Commissariat of Foreign Trade. In 1927, a police raid on its premises in London had led to a breaking off of diplomatic relations between the two countries that was to last till 1929. Thereafter, a keen desire on the British side to improve the balance of trade with the USSR made Arcos a busy company. The arrangements were quickly made. The sale was authorised in Protocol 150 of the Politburo of the Central Committee of the Communist Party of 5 December 1933, and duly signed by Secretary J. Stalin. The Codex was shipped by special courier over Christmas weekend, and reached Britain on Boxing Day. It spent the night in Bush House. On 27 December, fifteen minutes past noon and with a police escort, Mr Ernest Maggs walked into the Museum carrying the manuscript in a tin box wrapped in brown paper. The Director and Maggs checked the contents against the facsimile (three fragments were not present, but these were the parts recovered from bookbindings by Uspenski and therefore not part of the deal). A Pathe News movie shows them bending over the manuscript, treating it (one has to say) more roughly than would be tolerated nowadays.

Bush House, now the home of the BBC World Service, in 1933 was the headquarters of Arcos.

See Plate 16

Crowds (three thousand people) had turned up prematurely at the Museum on Boxing Day. On 28 December the queue stretched from the Reading Room entrance (where it was exhibited) to the main gates in Great Russell Street. *The Times* of 29 December reported that the 'crowd appeared to be drawn from all sorts and conditions of men and of women, and to be of many nations and languages. As they approached within sight of the shining parchment sheets, on which, under the electric light, the dark colour of the script – four columns to the page – showed up distinctly, not a few were moved out of reverence to take off their hats.'

In late January 1934, Archbishop Porphyrios of Sinai sent a telegram to London, asserting the Monastery's claim to be the 'sole rightful owner of the manuscript'. The British Museum replied the next day, rather unhelpfully referring him to the Soviet authorities. At the same time, Hill instigated an examination of the circum-stances under which the leaves now in London had left the Monastery. In fact there was little documentation available, except for published material. Copies of letters to Tischendorf from Archbishop Kallistratos were provided by Leipzig University Library within a few days, and shortly thereafter the Museum entered into correspondence about the available documentation with the grandson of Tischendorf, Walter Meyer van Bremen. In addition, advice was sought from the Attorney General, Lord Hanworth, who pronounced that the acquisition was legal.

THE APPEAL

The day of *The Times* report also saw the launch of the appeal, with a letter issued to the press from the Prime Minister, the Archbishop of Canterbury, M. R. James, Sir George Hill, Kenyon, and several other worthies. How to catch the public imagination was one preoccupation. John Johnson (a name to be seen on the printing details of books produced by Oxford University Press from 1926 to 1946) suggested calling the manuscript 'the oldest Family Bible or something like that'.

There were plenty of small donations. The collecting boxes at the Museum brought in between £20 and £40 a day, giving a total of £1,786 by the beginning of March. Matthew Black's lecture to an undergraduate class on important manuscripts always included a reference to his student donation of half-a-crown (a generous amount in 1934). In addition, facsimile pages (either single or a whole opening) were sold; one later given to my father is on my study wall. But £100,000 was going to take a lot of half-crowns (800,000, to be precise), and from the beginning big donors needed to be wooed. The Friends of the National Libraries in this the third year of its existence raised a substantial sum. Lord Wakefield gave an anonymous £1,000 donation as early as September 1933.

Viscount Wakefield of Castrol motor oil fame.

Differing views about the purchase reflect the tensions of the day. The press were divided, with *The Times*, the *Daily Telegraph*, the *Morning Post* and the BBC supportive, while other papers, including the Beaverbrook press, were hostile. Various old stories resurfaced. Simonides' claims to be the author of the Codex put some people off. Reports that the manuscript had been stolen from St Catherine's were refuted by Hill.

Some people were concerned that buying the manuscript from the Soviet Union was tantamount to endorsing a godless regime. Others believed that it was right to rescue a precious Christian artefact from the hands of the wicked. Hensley Henson, Bishop of Durham and opponent of trade unionism, gave £5 (perhaps not over-generous) and expressed his belief that the 'poorest as well as the more prosperous should be enabled to have a hand in what is nothing less than a national demonstration of our respect for that holy religion which the Atheists of Russia revile and seek to destroy'.

Other voices included the Association of British Creditors of Russia (which represented businesses which had lost their investments after the Revolution) and the Greek government (the ambassador promised to 'see how some Greek people may contribute to the fund').

Rather typically for the established church, it had been assumed that an appeal in the Church of England would do the job. This

The draft of this sentence contained a fine example of the way in which textual error arises: I initially wrote 'Maimonides' instead of 'Simonides'. My conscious mind had not thought of the medieval Jewish philosopher for a long time. I can think of no reasonable explanation why I should have written it. In the same way, at Matthew 13.54 Scribe A wrote 'Antipatris' instead of 'patris' ('home town'). But the claim that he wrote this because he was working somewhere close to Antipatris (a city near Caesarea) is as difficult to substantiate as would be the assumption that I was working on Maimonides at the time.

was unsatisfactory to the Free Churches, who were keen to make their own contribution. At a meeting of the National Council of Evangelical Churches in March, three priorities were named: supporting the purchase of Codex Sinaiticus, promoting world peace and restoring social services cut in the recession.

Pope Pius XI was invited to contribute, but his Holiness regretted that his English investments had depreciated, and assistance was beyond his command.

One voice we do not hear is that of the librarians in Leningrad. The campaign depicted the Soviet authorities as vandals in whose hands the manuscript was not safe (but its value was a good reason for looking after it well). The sale was beneficial to the government in Moscow, and to British culture. But its custodians and those in the Soviet Union who cared about such things must have regretted its departure.

The dealings and views of a number of great men have been recorded. But the most fitting conclusion to this section is to reproduce a letter from one E. B. Hooper to the Director of the British Museum dated 16 January 1934:

I am poor and I live in an attic, and – like others – I sent my tiny cheque (which was so small that of course it was not acknowledged; But people do what they can).

The appeal was wound up on 12 October 1935. Public subscriptions totalled £53,563. This, with the £7,000 given by the Trustees of the British Museum, left a bill of £39,437 to be footed by the taxpayer.

RESULTS OF THE ACQUISITION

The arrival of the manuscript provided the opportunity for a detailed examination. Two scholars were given the task. Both were Assistant Keepers in the Department of Manuscripts in the British Museum. H. J. M. Milne (1889–1965) had joined the department in 1912, and was an experienced and distinguished scholar whose publications included catalogues and a definitive work on ancient

Greek shorthand. T. C. Skeat (1907–2003) was the junior, having joined the library in 1931. He already had one significant publication to his name, the first edition of a papyrus manuscript containing sayings of Jesus, published under the title *Fragments of an Unknown Gospel*. Their research confounded the scepticism of those scholars who seemed to believe that there was nothing new to be discovered about Codex Sinaiticus. In a minute examination of the scribes and correctors, they proposed a radical simplification of the complicated schemata put forward by Tischendorf and Lake. It should be remembered that they had far greater access to the bulk of the manuscript than either of their predecessors, and they made good use of it in the four years after the manuscript arrived in London. Their descriptions of the hands at work on the manuscript, supported by a large collection of plates, remain fundamental to all research.

At the same time as the re-examination, the manuscript was rebound by Douglas Cockerell. Cockerell's elder brother Sydney had been assistant to William Morris for the last years of his life, and it was through him that Douglas went to be trained in traditional bookbinding by another follower of Morris and practitioner of the Arts and Crafts movement, T. J. Cobden-Sanderson. Out of this grew the Cockerell workshop in Grantchester, with a distinctive style of binding and design which reflect the proportions of the book. His *Bookbinding and the Care of Books* of 1901 is a classic work. His standing is shown by his selection for two significant projects: overseeing the printing and binding of the registers of the dead in all British First World War cemeteries; and rebinding the Codex Sinaiticus.

The detailed account of how this was done is not altogether pleasing to today's British Library conservators. It included placing the sheets flat on a frame, and attaching weights to them with bulldog clips in order to stretch them. But the binding itself, consisting of each testament in its own volume, with a cover of oak boards and white morocco, is extremely handsome. The leather has

Cockerell was later to rebind another biblical manuscript almost as old as Codex Sinaiticus, Codex Bezae.

a small degree of blind tooling inspired by early Coptic bindings (the closest available analogy). To avoid any of the parchment being hidden in the gutter, a linen guard was attached to each sheet, and the quires also were 'thrown out' to deal with the extra thickness of the volume caused by the guards. Something of the quality of the work may be gauged from the fact that the oak boards, only $\frac{3}{8}$ of an inch thick, have not warped.

SOURCES AND FURTHER READING

My principal debt in recounting the events of 1933–34 is to the researches by Dr William Frame of the British Library, and to his kindness in making his paper available to me.

For the account of Ernest Maggs's visit to Leningrad, see http://www.maggs.com/about/history.asp.

For Milne, see the obituary by Skeat in *The Times*, 18 February 1965.

The description of the rebinding of Codex Sinaiticus is from Milne and Skeat, *Scribes and Correctors*, pp. 83–86. It seems to have been provided by Cockerell.

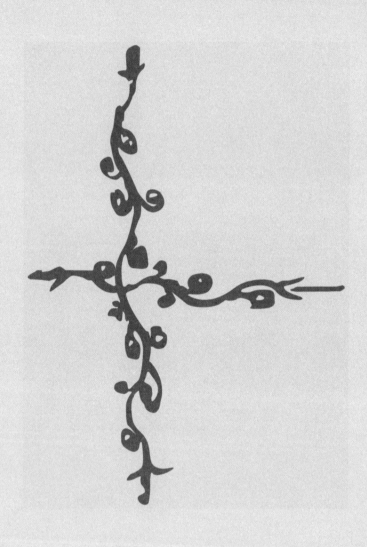

CHAPTER TWELVE

The Virtual Codex Sinaiticus

CODEX SINAITICUS was a very sophisticated production, which represented the most advanced technology of its day. Since then, book production has gone through a number of revolutions, and is currently in the middle of another. For the Greek book, one may single out three revolutions:

the transition from majuscule scripts to much smaller and more compact forms of writing, in the ninth to eleventh centuries

the replacement of manuscripts by printing with movable type, which was introduced to western Europe in the second half of the fifteenth century

the introduction of photographic facsimiles in the second half of the nineteenth century

Codex Sinaiticus has been affected by all three. The introduction of minuscule scripts led to a situation where nobody found majuscules easy or convenient to use. The wealth of aids for the reader which Byzantine readers of biblical manuscripts came to expect – accentuation, detailed punctuation, chapter titles, introductions and prefaces and lists of chapters and lections – were all absent here, so that it would have seemed a primitive and strange volume. The introduction of the printed book made possible a world of scholarship in which it was ultimately feasible for Tischendorf's transcription to be as near as possible a representation of Codex Sinaiticus. Rather than rendering the manuscript obsolete, it gave it new readers, even if they were readers at one remove from the manu-script itself. The facsimile edition of 1911 served exactly the same purpose, bringing the reader still closer to the manuscript.

Today we are in the early stages of the most momentous revolution since the days of Gutenberg and the pioneers of the Greek printed book, the invention of the electronic book, and in particular the web-based edition. The advantages of this new medium, and the ways in which it differs from and is similar to manuscript and print editions, will take some time to become clear. But there are some obvious points to mention.

ADVANTAGES FOR RESEARCH

Prior to the Project, access to Codex Sinaiticus was only possible in three ways, all of which were unsatisfactory. The oldest tool was the series of editions made by Tischendorf in the 1840s, which while remarkable achievements have various limitations. The second was the Lake facsimile, which by today's standards is limited in quality. Those who have seen several copies say that there is some variation between them. Both these productions also suffer from the dis-advantage of not containing parts of the manuscript discovered more recently. The third means of access is the least practical, namely to look at the manuscript itself. Quite apart from its dispersal across four countries, the librarians require very good reasons indeed before they will permit anyone to handle it, because of the risks of damage. I had a short time with the Leipzig leaves in May 1990. Only a handful of scholars have been allowed access to the London portion in the last generation. All three means of access are expensive and difficult for most people: the nineteenth-century edition and the photographic facsimile are rare, and even if seeing the manuscript were permitted, travel would require the commit-ment of resources.

A website surpasses these editions in accessibility. The Virtual Codex Sinaiticus makes the manuscript available globally to anyone with a browser. One does not need to travel to a library (or in this case to four libraries) in order to examine it; one has no need of any of the traditional panoply of resources needed by the student of ancient documents. In fact, such a website makes the study of an ancient text possible for people who so far have been quite without the opportunity to access it in any form. This project and others like it will have a significant effect not only in enhancing opportunities for all those interested in manuscripts, but also in creating new constituencies of users.

For those interested in academic study of the text, it makes new tools available to a much larger group. The result will be that anyone engaged in detailed research on the text of the Bible will be able to make use of images and transcriptions of one of the primary documents. As more manuscripts are made available digitally, scholars will be in a better position than ever before to understand how the Bible was copied and what its earliest forms were like. They will become less dependent on secondary sources of information provided by the few scholars who had access to the primary documents.

There will be several benefits for wider circles of people interested in the Bible either on account of their faith or out of cultural interest. One is that they will have equal access with the scholars to the primary material. They will not need to find an institution or join a library. Within the Churches, it seems likely that the autocracy of single forms of the text will be weakened. Access to ancient and differing forms of the Bible in our oldest manuscripts, with images and interpretative tools, will for Christianity (as for scholarship) lessen dependence on the secondary production of scholars. The opportunity is offered now to read parts of the Bible as they were available to the readers of Codex Sinaiticus in the fourth century.

The Virtual Codex Sinaiticus at www.sinaiticus.org therefore offers opportunities never before experienced. In this it is like Codex Sinaiticus itself, which also presented the Bible in a new way. And there are other similarities.

The first is that both the 'real' and the 'virtual' manuscripts have been produced by a team. In the fourth century, so large a task required sharing it out. Today, no individual possesses the full range of skills that are needed to create this website. As a team, both the original scribes and today's Project members have had similar tasks, notably determining technical standards and allotting responsibilities. The second is that both are projects which have used and adapted new technology and which have developed new concepts or modified existing ones. The third is that both are enterprises at the limits of what is possible in the scholarship and technology of their time. We have seen areas in which the scribes struggled to achieve their goal. The difficulties for the modern Project are not so obvious today. No doubt future generations will observe limitations in our use of our technology.

HISTORY

How do projects like this begin? Probably because several people have the same idea. In the case of Codex Sinaiticus, a number of events happily conspired to make it seem an obvious thing to do.

Fundamental to the Project are two matters. First and foremost is the conservation of the manuscript, all other considerations being secondary to this. Given the very high scientific standards of principles and recording achieved in modern conservation, the importance of a consistent approach to all parts of the manuscript was becoming increasingly obvious. The second has been the opportunity to apply new technology, above all in making high-quality digital images, and secondarily in making an electronic transcription of the text.

The ground was also prepared by activity not necessarily related to Codex Sinaiticus. Digital imaging of manuscripts in the library at St Catherine's had, thanks to the vision and energy of Archbishop Damianos, begun in the mid 1990s, and experts such as Nicholas Pickwoad of the Camberwell College of Arts and the freelance digitisation specialist David Cooper played a key role in supporting the monastery in developing this essential work. Research partnerships and personal contacts therefore provided a natural setting for extending this success to Codex Sinaiticus, while conservation and imaging laid the foundation for what was to follow. But it was textual scholars who came up with suggestions that set the ball rolling.

The development of web-based electronic editions of manuscripts is very recent indeed. The World Wide Web only came into being in 1993. The same year saw a prospectus for an electronic edition (on CD-ROM) of *Beowulf*, an Anglo-Saxon poem surviving in an eleventh-century copy in the British Library. The core of the edition consists of images of each page of the manuscript, with a full electronic transcription. The subsequent success of this edition convinced the British Library of the importance of digital media for recording its collections and making them available. At the same time, New Testament textual scholarship was dipping its toes in the same water. Confronted with vast amounts of data, and frustrated by the limitations of trying to understand and manipulate it all on paper, the use of computers offered schemes for controlling the material and presenting far more of it than would be available in a print edition. From 1997, two leading research groups began to collaborate in editing the text. They were the International Greek New Testament Project and the Institute for New Testament Textual Research, Münster, Germany. The International Greek New Testament Project is a largely Anglo-American team, founded in 1949. In recent decades it has been based at the University of Birmingham in the UK. The Institute for New Testament Textual Research, founded in 1959 by Kurt Aland, has been responsible for many of the basic tools of New Testament research, in particular the most widely used edition of the Greek New Testament. The two groups began to cooperate with a pioneer in making digital editions, Peter Robinson. His Canterbury Tales Project adopts the concept that the entire edition is based upon complete transcriptions of all the manuscripts which, accompanied by images, give the user full access to the primary documents.

The results of these partnerships may be seen at www.igntp.org and www.uni-muenster.de/INTF/

At the same time, Amy Myshrall was writing a doctoral thesis in Birmingham on Codex Sinaiticus and its correctors in the Gospels. In retrospect, it seems inevitable that she should have raised with me the idea of making an electronic edition of Codex Sinaiticus. The British Library's Dr Scot McKendrick and I then met in the Library on 1 November 2001 to discuss the idea further.

Independently, Professor Robert Littman of the University of Hawaii was working on the Septuagint of Tobit. Septuagint studies has hitherto invested less in electronic resources. But it has its own major projects, including an ongoing critical edition based in Göttingen, and several translation projects into modern languages. Frustrated by the limitations of current resources for studying Codex Sinaiticus, Littman also proposed the idea of an online edition to the British Library in 2001.

It turned out that in the Library they had already been discussing the value of making digital images of their leaves, and so we were able immediately to agree to pursue the Project. The next twelve months consisted of planning within the Library and tentative discussions, leading to an approach to the future partners and other interested parties in early September 2002. The first meeting to involve a wider group of potential participants was held at the British Library on 7 November 2002.

Thereafter things developed very fast, with the identification of the separate parts of the Project, the creation of a timetable, the formation of a structure, and the beginnings of fundraising. Throughout, permanent staff at the British Library with expertise in the different areas required, including project organisation, publications, fundraising, conservation, imaging and expertise in Greek manuscripts, played key roles in developing and running the Project. Dr Claire Breay was Project Manager from the beginning, with Dr William Frame and Dr Juan Garcés, the Project Curator from 2006, taking her place when she was on leave. Dr Scot McKendrick was intimately involved in all aspects of the Project, both intellectually and practically.

Central to the entire Project has been the leadership of the four partner institutions. The role of all other participating groups and individuals has been to provide specialist expertise. It is here worth pointing again to the importance of world politics in the history of Codex Sinaiticus. The reunification of Germany and the subsequent rejuvenation of Leipzig University Library, partially in ruins since 1945, meant that the Leipzig leaves of the Codex were able to play an important symbolic role in the library's engagement in international partnership. Easier correspondence with Russia was to make possible the examination of the documents relating to the donation of 1869, as well as no less symbolically combining the material found by Tischendorf with the fragments taken by his rival Uspenski. The discovery at St Catherine's Monastery of leaves and fragments of Codex Sinaiticus among the New Finds, and the current cataloguing and imaging work being carried on in the library, completed the set of opportunities for new partnerships.

The structure consisted of a Project Board, and a number of working parties dealing with conservation, imaging, the transcription, translations, the scholarly content of the Project, the website and various practical aspects of the Project.

One of the first tasks of each group was to agree technical standards, to be applied throughout the Project regardless of the various geographical locations of the manuscript.

FUNDING AND SCHOLARLY NETWORKS

So complex and ambitious a project, producing a free-to-view website, requires ambitious funding. Evidently, the four partner institutions made significant contributions of their own resources in setting it all in motion and maintaining it, as did other groups such as the Münster Institut. Within that framework, a number of sources contributed to different aspects of the Project. The website was designed and built with funding from the Deutsche Forschungsgemeinschaft, the German national funding body. The transcription and alignment was funded by the Arts and Humanities Research

Council, the equivalent body in the UK. A number of private foundations also contributed generously, namely the Stavros Niarchos Foundation, the Leventis Foundation, the Mariposa Foundation, the Chandris Foundation, the J. F. Costopoulos Foundation, the Hellenic Foundation, the American Friends of Saint Catherine's Monastery and the American Trust for the British Library.

Other organisations contributed their support in different ways. The Society of Biblical Literature (the world's largest such organisation, with 9,000 members, over half of whom attend its annual congress in the USA) provided encouragement and a forum for presentations, and sent its president to Project Board meetings. The Göttinger Digitalisierungszentrum (Centre for Retrospective Digitisation), Göttingen State and University Library, Germany offered its expertise.

Many individuals have given their time to the Project: conservators, digitisers and technical experts in various fields, historians, textual scholars and translators. Their names are listed on the Project website. Some of their work is acknowledged in the previous pages. Together, the collaboration between libraries, other institutions and many individuals (some of which may have had no particular reason to work together), has made the Project a success in more than its declared goals. It represents all that is best about the ability of people to work together towards a common goal, and demonstrates the wider value of scholarly enterprises.

CONSERVATION

The primary responsibility of every library must be the conservation of its holdings. The first task of the Project was therefore a conservation assessment of the manuscript. It began in the British Library (which after all has the largest number of leaves to look after). A schedule was drawn up of the desiderata in a detailed conservation study. This included recording data about the parchment and its preparation, the degree of use and any damage, and remains of earlier bindings, for every leaf in the manuscript.

Hundreds of digital photographs of details were taken with a hand-held camera. The assessment has set new standards for the conservation of ancient documents. It will take some time to analyse all the data, but it has the potential to cast fresh light on ancient manuscript production.

The conservation of the Old Testament British Library leaves took place between October 2005 and March 2006, and of the New Testament leaves between September and December 2006. Necessary repairs (which were kept to a minimum) of each section were carried out after completion of the assessment.

Once the conservation was complete, and there was no danger of any damage being made worse, it was possible to move on to the next stage.

IMAGING

The technical standards were the highest possible. There was also a greater challenge, namely that of imposing the same standards in four different locations so as to achieve a uniform result.

For the technically minded, the selected equipment used at the British Library consisted of:

PowerPhase and *PowerPhase FX* digital scanning backs
TG1 Filter/AR1 Filter
DeVere 480 rostrum camera
Rodenstock Apo–Sironar f90/135mm lens

The *PowerPhase FX* digital camera back employs a $10,500 \times 12,600$ pixel CCD chip that enables image captures of 380 MB (24 bit RGB uninterpolated). Sironar digital lenses were chosen for their greater depth of field, giving better focus for bound materials, as well as conservation benefits because no mounting with glass plates or clips is required. Standard fluorescent cold lighting was used, again with the welfare of the manuscript in mind. A machine creating a slight vacuum was used to keep the pages flat while they were being scanned.

The first stage was to make various trials and to assess the results. We met a number of times in the spring of 2006. The first images were taken using very strong light, with the result that the writing from the other side of the page being imaged (or even from the level beyond that) was almost as visible as the page being photographed. Lowering the light level and using backing paper solved that problem. But the type of backing paper affected the colour of the parchment. It was either too creamy, or too grey, or too white. After a number of attempts, we selected a colour which kept something of the warmth of the manuscript's own colour, while providing a contrast with the ink.

What is the manuscript's own colour? We looked at the British Library leaves only by artificial light, while the differing storage conditions and environment in Leipzig, St Petersburg and Sinai give it a different appearance in each place.

THE OTHER LOCATIONS

Conservation and imaging in Leipzig and St Petersburg followed the same procedures and documentation in conservation of the manuscript. In fact, all conservation was carried out in the presence of staff who had been involved in the British Library assessment, to ensure consistency of practice. Imaging in St Petersburg was carried out in 2008 by the same photographer (Laurence Pordes). The Leipzig images, taken by a different team using different equipment, of leaves which had existed under different conditions since 1844, produced rather different-looking results (compare Q34-F8v and Q35-F1r). Imaging was carried out at St Catherine's in the summer of 2008 by Michael Phelps, using the monastery's new Stokes Imaging digital camera and cradle.

Every page was imaged in two ways: 'normally', using light shining onto the surface from a broad angle; and with 'raking light', the light sources being at such an oblique angle that many features in the surface of the parchment are shown very clearly by their shadow. The technique is similar to aerial photographs, which often reveal most about a landscape's development when they are taken early in the morning or close to sunset.

In addition, some difficult pages were selected for imaging using ultraviolet light. Experiments using multi-spectral imaging (searching an area with light from varying points in the spectrum, by which it is possible to detect ink visible at one point in the spectrum but not another) were disappointing. Ultraviolet, which was used to good effect by Milne and Skeat, is sometimes able to reveal text subsequently washed out or erased.

TRANSCRIPTION

Conservation, imaging and transcription were the three essential parts of the Project for making as complete a record of the manuscript as possible. Of the three, transcription was the most time-consuming.

There are two challenges in making an electronic transcription. The first is identical with that faced by the scribes of Codex Sinaiticus: accuracy in representation of the copy. It is arguable that what the transcribers produced is an electronic manuscript which, while intended to be a precise reproduction, is in fact a fresh step in the tradition, on a par with any (lost) manuscripts which were copied from Codex Sinaiticus in antiquity. But the user expects it to contain the same text as Codex Sinaiticus.

The best way to achieve the greatest possible accuracy is by making independent transcriptions, automatically generating a list of the differences, and then verifying the correct one. For the Old Testament and Barnabas and Hermas, we made two transcriptions, one with page layout and one without. These transcriptions were made by taking an existing electronic version and changing it to reproduce Codex Sinaiticus. The only exception to this was Hermas, for which the text had to be keyed in from the manuscript.

For the New Testament, the process was more complicated. The foundation was a complete transcription made at the Institute for New Testament Textual Research for the online edition called New Testament Prototypes, which may be seen on the institute's website. Again, it was produced from two independent transcriptions. The transcription of John has a more complicated history. The Münster version uses a transcription made for the International Greek New

The lilies of the field correction and the initial omission of the ending of John are visible only with ultraviolet lighting.

See above for the website address.

Testament Project. This included information about the corrections provided by T. C. Skeat, who possessed a detailed recollection of his examination of the manuscript sixty years earlier.

Possessing an electronic starting point, and in the case of the New Testament, an existing transcription, was essential to the success of the Project. Even so, the task of reading and encoding most of the Bible, along with layout and over 20,000 corrections, was a remarkable achievement, carried out as it was by two people over the course of two years. These are the only two people who have read every word of what is now extant in Codex Sinaiticus *and* examined leaves in all four locations.

From manuscript to web

The basic transcriptions are all what are known as plain text files. The following shows the first verse of John's Gospel.

```
|Q 80-1r|
{-fn- 247}
{-qs 1- οθ}
|C 1|
|L|–B 36• –K 0• –V 0• [app][S1]κατα ïωαννην[\S1][*]OM[\*][\app]
|L|–K 1• –V 1• [eus]α-γ[\eus] ᾽outd εν αρχη ην ο λογοσ
|L|και ο λογοσ ην
|L|προσ τον θν και
|L|θσ ην ο λογοσ –V 2• ου=
```

This is no use to anyone except the transcription team. So it is turned into XML (Extensible Markup Language), so that the first part of it looks like this:

```
<div id="B-B36K0V0-36-JOHN" n="36" type="book" title="Κατὰ Ἰωάννην"><div id="K-B36K0V0-36-JOHN" n="0" type="chapter"><ab id="V-B36K0V0-36-JOHN" n="0"><pb id="S-80-1r" corres="E-80-1r" n="80-1r" scribeid="A" archive="BL" localfol="247"><margin type="topmargin"><margin type="marginright"><note type="folionum">247</note><note type="quireSig" n="79">οθ</note></margin>
```

```
</margin>
</pb>
<cb id="S-80-1r-1" corres="E-80-1r-1" n="1"><margin type=
"coltopmargin"><margin type="center"><note type="booktitle">
<app><rdg type="corr" n="S1"><w n="1">κατα</w> <w n=
"2">ϊωαννην</w></rdg><rdg type="main-corr"><w n="1">
</w></rdg></app></note></margin></margin></cb>
<lb id="S-80-1r-1-1" corres="E-80-1r-1-1" n="1" rend="hang"
vnumber="1:1"><margin><note type="ECN" Ammonian=
"1" Canon="3"><hi rend="red"><hi rend="ol2">α</hi>
<lb />γ</hi></note></margin></lb></ab></div>
<div id="K-B36K1V1-36-JOHN" n="1" type="chapter">
<ab id="V-B36K1V1-36-JOHN" n="1"> <w n="1">εν</w>
<w n="2">αρχη</w> <w n="3">ην</w> <w n=
"4">ο</w> <w n="5">λογοc </w> <lb id="E-80-1r-1-1"
corres="S-80-1r-1-1"/>
```

The XML for the entire transcription contains many millions of characters (that for John alone contains, including spaces, 1,225,291). This process also converts the original text files into Unicode, the international encoding system whose remit is to give a unique identifier to every symbol in every language.

Even this is not enough, and a further stage of conversion (to HTML) has to take place before the transcription can be viewed on the website.

At first glance, both transcription and XML seem a world away from the production of Codex Sinaiticus. But the similarities are more important. The tagging has the same purpose as the consistency of presentation shown by the scribes and the ways the correctors found of making their changes: to ensure that what the reader sees is always what should be seen, that it is in the right place, and that it is clear.

Alignment

The way in which the transcription was made follows a system developed over more than a decade of making such transcriptions of New Testament manuscripts, extended to provide more detail. The alignment, on the other hand, represents a new advance. It was devised by Peter Robinson and Andrew West, and adapts existing software. The program recognises units down to the level of the line. The linking of the individual words was carried out manually by postgraduates at the University of Birmingham.

The alignment system allows users of all levels of knowledge and experience to explore the development of the manuscript in more detail. It is a way of showing how the text is presented; it provides a medium for learning how to read the script of Codex Sinaiticus; it interprets the corrections and other textual and paratextual elements; it indicates to the expert how the team has interpreted ambiguous or disputed material.

INTERPRETATIVE MATERIAL

Images and transcription on their own are valuable for a small body of experts. But for most people (including those experts), interpretation is essential, for several reasons. One of them is that, in the course of the Project, the team has learned a great deal about Codex Sinaiticus. This information should be recorded before it is forgotten. Another reason is that since one of the Project's aims is to share the study of a great manuscript with new and diverse audiences, supporting material is essential. Such material takes several forms, including information about the manuscript, discussions of key points and images of details and translations.

Translations

A complete translation of the entire manuscript presented several difficulties: first, there are plenty of places where the unique wording of Codex Sinaiticus cannot be represented in translation; second, it would be very expensive; third, the selection of a single language would be invidious. The decision was therefore taken to include excerpts in various languages. These excerpts are intended to give the flavour of the whole. The translation of the Septuagint provides an opportunity to experience the distinctive features of the version.

DEVISING THE WEBSITE

The development of the website was the primary responsibility of Leipzig University Library, and included support from the German government's research funding body. After tenders, the company ACS Solutions, a firm specialising in IT services and based in Leipzig, was selected to carry out the design. The work was led by Mustafa Dogan (and subsequently by Leander Seige) at Leipzig University Library in partnership with the IT Department of Leipzig University. Beyond initial design, the website needed to cater for the varied demands of those producing image files, transcriptions, alignment files, translations, the conservation report and content.

ROLLING OUT THE PROJECT WEBSITE

Given the varied demands, and the difficulty of synchronising conservation, imaging, transcription, delivery and making everything work, the website was launched in three phases. The first was hosted at Leipzig University Library. It consisted of the images, transcription and conservation report relating to three classes of material:

> all the forty-three leaves in Leipzig University Library (Codex Friderico-Augustanus)
> the remaining leaves of the books represented among the Leipzig leaves (one leaf of 1 Chronicles, the rest of Jeremiah)
> the Psalms and the Gospel of Mark

It also included an English translation of some psalms and a limited amount of other content.

The site was launched on 24 July 2008, with a press conference in Leipzig University Library and a live link to the British Library. The first two days saw a minimum of 117,000 visitors and more than ten million hits.

Phase 2 was published on 21 November of the same year, at the Society of Biblical Literature meeting in Boston, Massachusetts, with the addition of more Old Testament leaves in London and St Petersburg, further leaves being added in subsequent weeks.

Phase 3 was completed on 6 July 2009. It consisted of the publication of the rest of the New Testament with Barnabas and Hermas and the New Finds fragments. Further content and translations were added at the same time. By the end of the summer the website had received over one million visitors.

A CONFERENCE

The Project has produced a huge amount of published material. But what has been made available does not represent all of what has been learned. There have been many skills and techniques either developed or honed: new software, new concepts of what an electronic version of an ancient manuscript could be, new standards in digitising and in conservation, discoveries about the manuscript's manufacture and its history. The July 2009 conference at the British Library, at which the publication of all the images and transcription was celebrated, provided an occasion for those who had worked on it to share what they had learned with a wider audience, and for other scholars to present their own research on the manuscript.

A second conference was held in St Petersburg in November 2009.

A BOOK

So much is now known about Codex Sinaiticus, and the Project offers the raw materials for so much more research, that a stream of scholarly publications should follow, leading to fresh evaluations of a number of aspects of manuscript and biblical research. A less specialist book has two purposes: it gives a researcher a broad description which will suggest areas where further work is awaited, and it shares scholarship with a wide audience.

It does not do so by simplifying, but by describing an entire topic from a single perspective. This book has been written by someone involved with the Project from its conception. To speak personally, the study of the manuscripts is essential to a proper understanding of any text. When one is dealing with a tradition as long and as complex and as rich as that of the biblical books, that study is even more important. It brings home the significance of its physical manifestation for how the text is understood. Codex Sinaiticus is not only one of the most magnificent of manuscripts, and one of the oldest codices; its continuing existence, and the wider influence it will have now that it is accessible to more people than ever before, is a testimony to the textual diversity that is one of the riches of the biblical tradition. Leather scrolls, papyrus scrolls and codices, parchment codices and then paper codices, printed books using ever more sophisticated machinery, and now electronic books: these are a remarkable variety of media for a couple of collections of ancient Hebrew and Greek writings. Together, they are our evidence that those writings existed in a variety of forms which continued to develop over centuries, a testimony to the wealth of interpretations and intellectual developments that engaged with them and in-fluenced them. The handwritten Codex Sinaiticus is one of the most important copies, made at one of the most important stages in the whole history of copying, and is one of the most important survivals from the past. What role will the digital Codex Sinaiticus play in the future of the biblical text? The most exciting thing is that we do not know. As we complete this online edition, almost precisely 150 years after Tischendorf's dramatic third visit to St Catherine's, we can be sure of the continuing power of the real Codex Sinaiticus and its history to fascinate and to inspire.

SOURCES AND FURTHER READING

The sources for this chapter are the documentation of the Project itself, much of which is available on the Codex Sinaiticus website.

There is a short account in S. McKendrick and J. Garcés, 'The Codex Sinaiticus Project: 1. The Book and the Project', in G. Fellows-Jensen and P. Springborg (eds), *Care and Conservation of Manuscripts 10: Proceedings of the Tenth International Seminar held at the University of Copenhagen 19th–20th October 2006*, Copenhagen: Museum Tusculanum Press, 2008, pp. 148–52. See also the article by Dr Ekkehard Henschke, who as Leipzig University Librarian until 2005 played a key role in setting up the Project, 'Digitising the Hand-Written Bible: The Codex Sinaiticus, its History and Modern Presentation', *Libri. International Journal of Libraries and Information Services*, 57 (2007), pp. 45–51.

For the history of electronic editions of the New Testament, and their relationship to manuscript copies and earlier editions such as those of Tischendorf, see Chapter Six of my book *An Introduction to the New Testament Manuscripts and their Texts*, Cambridge: Cambridge University Press, 2008.

APPENDIX

Exploring the Website

THIS book has been written so that it may be read without the website. The following paragraphs suggest ways in which exploring the images, transcription, conservation document and other features may enrich the book, and the reader's understanding of the manuscript. Use of the website will also explain the claims that have been made above for the digital edition.

THE TRANSCRIPTION

To start with, go to 'See the Manuscript', and turn on the image and transcription. Click the mouse over any word in the original columns of the manuscript in either the image or the transcription, and the same word will be highlighted in the other. This will also work if you have the image on high magnification, and need to look at a particular place: click the mouse over the word you want to see, and the image will move to that place. This tool gives a way of learning to read the manuscript. Since it is written in what today are called capital letters, without word breaks, with very little punctuation, and without modern chapter divisions or verse divisions, the transcription (which contains all these features) functions as a tool for finding one's way around the manuscript.

But it also functions as an explanation of the detail, especially of the corrections. Every corrected word is shown in a different colour (blue at the time of writing), and pointing the mouse at that word will give a pop-up box containing the correction and indicating which corrector made it. Some of these corrections are placed in the top, bottom or side margin, and are one of the most obvious features which a visitor will see in the manuscript. So the transcription also places these corrections in the matching place, as well as in the place where it is inserted.

In practice some limitation became necessary, and of additions in the side margins only those of four or more words in length are included.

THE IMAGES

Exploring the images, the detail visible in the writing is stunning. One can see how each letter was formed. Using the raking light images, one can sometimes almost see the ink in relief on the page, and many details of the surface emerge. It is worth remembering that the scribes wrote with no expectation that their characters would be held up for such detailed scrutiny, magnified far beyond their original size. But the consistency of stroke and of letter shape stands up to this examination extremely well. It would be a slight exaggeration to say that one can see more in the images than in the manuscript itself. Certainly the experts who made the transcription did go to the libraries to check some difficult places. But for most purposes, the images, especially if one takes the direct and raking light together, provide adequate access.

Use of the images and transcription together is a way of developing fluency in reading biblical majuscule and understanding the distinctive features of a manuscript, as well as those peculiar to Codex Sinaiticus.

THE CONSERVATION ASSESSMENT

Another way to explore the images is by using the Conservation Assessment. With image and Physical Description turned on, the image will be displayed with red lines dividing it into a number of zones. The assessment's comments on a wide range of features, including the preparation of the page for writing, binding, state of repair, and pricking and ruling, contain links to the zones of the image to which they relate, so that one can easily find one's way to them.

THE TRANSLATIONS

The translations may be viewed on their own, or with images, transcription or both. Using them with the images offers a way of exploring the corrections, since those which can be translated into another language are noted (changes to spelling and grammatical corrections cannot always be represented). Using them with either image or transcription (or both) is a useful tool for someone developing their understanding of Greek.

INDEX OF REFERENCES TO THE BOOKS IN CODEX SINAITICUS

according to the order in which the Codex contained them

INDEX OF NAMES
AND SUBJECTS

Page numbers in italic refer to Sources and Further Reading

CΗCΟΠΟΥΚΛΙΕ
ΦΑΓΟΝΑΡΤΟΝΕΥ
ΧΑΡΙCΤΗCΑΝΤΟC
ΤΟΥΚΥΚΑΙΑΛΟΝΤ
ΟΤΙΟΥΚΗΝΕΚΕΙ
ICΟΥΔΕΟΙΜΑΘΗ
ΤΑΙΑΝΕΒΗCΑΝΕΙ
ΤΟΠΛΟΙΟΝΚΑΙΝΑ
ΘΟΝΕΙCΚΑΦΑΡΝΑ
ΟΥΜΖΗΤΟΥΝΤΕ
ΤΟΝΙΗΚΑΙΕΥΡΟΝ
ΤΕCΑΥΤΟΝΠΕΡΑΝ
ΤΗCΘΑΛΑCCHCEI
ΠΟΝΑΥΤΩΡΑΒΒΙ
ΠΟΤΕΩΔΕΛΗΛΥΘΑC
ΑΠΕΚΡΙΘΗΑΥΤΟΙC
ICΚΑΙΕΙΠΕΝΑΜΗ
ΑΜΗΝΛΕΙCYΜΙΝ
ΟΥΧΟΤΙΕΙΔΕΤΕΗ
ΜΙΑΛΛΟΤΙΕΦΑ
ΤΕΕΚΤΩΝΑΡΤΩΝ
ΚΑΙΕΧΟΡΤΑCΘΗ
ΤΕ
ΕΡΓΑΖΕCΘΕΒΡΩ
ΜΗΝΤΗΝΑΠΟΛΛY
ΜΕΝΗΝΑΛΛΑΤΗ
ΜΕΝΟΥCΑΝΕΙC
ΗΝΑΙΩΝΙΟΝΗΝ
ΟΥΙΟCΤΟΥΑΝΘ
ΠΟΥΔΙΑΩCΙΝΥΜ
ΤΟΥΤΟΝΓΑΡΟΠΑΤΗ
ΟΘΕ ΟΕ ΟΥΝ
ΠΡΟCΑΥΤΟΝΤΙΠ
ΩΜΕΝΙΝΕΡΓΑΖΩ
ΜΕΘΑΤΑΕΡΓΑΤΟΥ
ΑΠΕΚΡΙΘΗ ΙC ΚΑΙ
ΠΕΝΑΥΤΟΙCΤΟΥ
ΤΟΕCΤΙΝΤΟΕΡΓΟΝ
ΤΟΥΘΥ ΙΝΑΠΙCΤΥ
ΗΤΑΙΕΙCΟΝΑΠΕ
ΛΕΝΕΚΕΙΝΟCΕΙ
ΠΟΝΟΥΝΑΥΤΩ
ΤΙΠΟΙΕΙCCΗΜΙ
CΥΙΝΑΙΔΩΜΕΝ
ΚΑΙΠΙCΤΕΥCΩΜΕ
COIΤΙΕΡΓΑΖΗΟΙ
ΠΑΤΕΡΕCΗΜΩΝ
ΤΟΜΑΝΝΑΕΦΑ

ΕΝΤΗΕΡΗΜΩΚΑ
ΘΩCΕCΤΙΝΓΕΓΡΑ
ΜΕΝΟΝΕΚΤΟΥΟΥ
ΡΑΝΟΥΕΔΩΚΕΝ
ΑΥΤΟΙCΦΑΓΕΙΝΕΙ
ΠΕΝΟΥΝΑΥΤΟΙC
ΙС
ΑΜΗΝΑΜΗΝΛΕΓ
ΥΜΙΝΟΥΜΩΥCΗ
ΔΕΔΩΚΕΝΥΜΙΝ
ΤΟΝΑΡΤΟΝΕΚΤΟΥ
ΟΥΡΑΝΟΥΑΛΛΟ
ΠΑΤΗΡΜΟΥΔΙΔΩ
CΙΝΥΜΙΝΤΟΝΑΡ
ΤΟΝΕΚΤΟΥΟΥΡΑ
ΝΟΥΤΟΝΑΛΗΘΙ
ΟΓΑΡΑΡΤΟCΤΟΥ
ΘΥΕCΤΙΝΟΚΑΤΑ
ΒΑΙΝΩΝΕΚΤΟΥ
ΡΑΝΟΥΚΑΙΖΩΗ
ΔΙΔΟΥCΤΩΚΟCΜ
ΕΙΠΟΝΟΥΝΠΡΟC
ΑΥΤΟΝΠΑΝΤΟΤΕ
ΚΕΛΟCΗΜΙΝΤΟΝ
ΑΡΤΟΝΤΟΥΤΟΝ
ΕΙΠΕΝΟΥΝΑΥΤΟΙC
ΟΙCΕΓΩΕΙΜΙΟΑΡ
ΤΟCΤΗCΖΩΗCΟ
ΕΡΧΟΜΕΝΟCΠΡ
ΕΜΕΟΥΜΗΠΕΙΝΑ
CΗΚΑΙΟΠΙCΤΕΥ
ΩΝΕΙCΕΜΕΟΥΜΗ
ΔΙΨΗCΕΙΠΩΠΟΤΕ
ΑΛΛΕΙΠΟΝΥΜΙΝ
ΟΤΙΚΑΙΕΩΡΑΚΑΤ
ΚΑΙΟΥΠΙCΤΕΥΕ
ΠΑΝΟΔΙΔΩCΙΝ
ΜΟΙΟΠΑΤΗΡΠΡ
ΕΜΕΝΗΞΕΙΚΑΙΤΟΝ
ΕΡΧΟΜΕΝΟΝΠΡ
ΕΜΕΟΥΜΗΕΚΒΑΛ
ΟΤΙΟΥΚΑΤΑΒΕΒΗ
ΚΑΕΚΤΟΥΟΥΡΑΝΟΥ
ΙΝΑΠΟΙΗCΩΤΟ
ΘΕΛΗΜΑΤΟΕΜΟΝ
ΑΛΛΑΤΟΘΕΛΗΜΑ
ΤΟΥΠΕΜ-ΑΝΤΟC
ΜΕΙΝΑΓΑΝΟΝ

ΔΩΚΕΝΜΟΙΜΗΔ
ΠΟΛΕCΩΕΞΑΥΤ
ΑΛΛΑΝΑCΤΗCΩ
ΑΥΤΟΕΝΤΗΕCΧΑ
ΤΗΗΜΕΡΑΤΟΥΤ
ΓΑΡΕCΤΙΝΤΟΘΕΛΗ
ΜΑΤΟΥΠΑΤΡΟCΜ
ΙΝΑΠΑCΟΘΕΩΡ
ΤΟΝΥΝΚΑΙΠΙCΤΕ
ΩΝΕΙCΑΥΤΟΝΕΧ
ΖΩΗΝΑΙΩΝΙΟΝ
ΚΑΙΑΝΑCΤΗCΩΑΥ
ΤΟΝΕΓΩΕΝΤΗΕCΧ
ΤΗΗΜΕΡΑ
ΕΓΟΓΓΥΖΟΝΟΥΝΟΙ
ΙΟΥΔΑΙΟΙΠΕΡΙΑΥ
ΤΟΥΟΤΙΕΙΠΕΝΕ
ΕΙΜΙΟΑΡΤΟCΟΚΑ
ΤΑΒΑCΕΚΤΟΥΟΥΡΑ
ΝΟΥΚΑΙΕΛΕΓΟΝ
ΟΥΧΟΥΤΟCΕCΤΙΝ
ΙCΟΥCΙΩCΗΦΟΥ
ΗΜΙCΟΙΔΑΜΕΝ
ΤΟΝΠΑΤΕΡΑΚΑΙΤΩ
ΟΥΝΟΥΤΟCΛΕΓΕΙ
ΟΤΙΕΚΤΟΥΟΥΡΑΝ
ΚΑΤΑΒΕΒΗΚΑ
ΑΠΕΚΡΙΘΗΟΥΝΙC
ΤΟΙCΚΑΙΕΙΠΕΝΜΗ
ΓΟΓΓΥΖΕΤΑΙΜΕ
ΛΗΝΑ ΟΥΔΙCΔΥ
ΝΑΤΑΙΕΛΘΙΝΠΡ
ΜΕΕΑΝΜΗΟΠΑ
ΤΗΡΟΠΕΜ-ΑCΜ
ΕΛΚΥCΗΑΥΤΟΝΚΑ
ΓΩΑΝΑCΤΗCΩ
ΤΟΝΤΗΕCΧΑΤΗ
ΜΕΡΑ
ΕCΤΙΓΕΓΡΑΜΜΕΝ
ΕΝΤΟΙCΠΡΟΦΗΤΑΙ
ΚΑΙΕCΟΝΤΑΙΠΑΝ
ΤΕCΔΙΔΑΚΤΟΙΘΥ
ΠΑCΟΑΚΟΥCΑCΠΑ
ΡΑΤΟΥΠΑΤΡΟCΚΑ
ΜΑΘΩΝΕΡΧΕΤΑΙ
ΠΡΟCΕΜΕΟΥΧ
ΤΙΤΟΝΠΑΤΕΡΑΕΩ
ΡΑΚΕΝΤΙCΕΙΜΗ

ΩΝΠΑΡΑΤΟΥ
ΥΤΟCΕΩΡΑ
ΤΟΝΠ ΤΗ
ΑΜΗΝΑΜΗ
ΥΜΙΝΟΤΙΟΠΙ
ΩΝΕΧΕΙΖΩ
ΑΙΩΝΙΟΝΕ
ΜΙΟΑΡΤΟCΤΗ
ΗCΟΙΠΑΤΕΡΕ
ΜΩΝΕΦΑΓΟ
ΜΑΝΝΑΕΝΤ
ΜΩΚΑΙΑΠΕΘ
ΟΥΤΟCΕCΤΙ
ΤΟCΕΚΤΟΥΟΥ
ΝΟΥΚΑΙΑΒΑ
ΙΝΑΤΙCΕΞΑ
ΦΑΓΗΚΑΙΜΗ
ΘΑΝΗ
ΕΓΩΕΙΜΙΟΑΡ
ΖΩΝΟΕΚΤΟΥ
ΡΑΝΟΥΚΑΤΑΒ
ΑΝΤΙCΦΑΓΗ
ΕΜΟΥΤΟΥ
ΕICΤΟΝΑΙΩ
ΑΡΤΟCΟΝΕΓ
CΩΥΠΕΡΤΗC
ΚΟCΜΟΥΖΩΗ
CΑΡΞΜΟΥΕCΤ
ΕΜΑΧΟΝΤΟΟ
ΑΛΛΗΛΟΥCΟΙ
ΑΙΟΙΛΕΓΟΝ
ΠΩCΟΥΝΑΥΤ
ΗΜΙΝΟΥΤΟC
ΝΑΓΙΝΦΑΓ
ΓΙΝ
ΕΙΠΕΝΟΥΝΑΥ
ΟΙCΑΜΗΝΑΜ
ΛΕΓΩΥΜΙΝΑ
ΦΑΓΗΤΑΙΤΗ
ΚΑΤΟΥ ΥΥΤΟ
ΕΡΠΟΥΚΑΙ
ΠΕΤΟΑΙΜΑΑΛΛ
ΟΥΚΕΧΕΤΕΖ
ΑΙΩΝΙΟΝΕΝ
ΤΟΙC
ΟΤΡΩΓΩΝΜΟ
CΑΡΚΑΚΑΙΠΙ
ΜΟΥΤΟΑΙΜΑ